The Democratic Republic of the Congo

THE DEMOCRATIC REPUBLIC OF THE CONGO is a mixture of all the adventure, mystery, and beauty described by writers of the last century and a modern technological society of the twentieth century. In this book Louise Crane, born and raised in the Congo, provides an historical base of its colonial beginnings to further the understanding of this rapidly emerging African nation.

The Congo, with its capital at Kinshasha, is rich in natural resources and its people are an energetic population with a varied heritage of customs and traditions. This combination has contributed to The Democratic Republic of the Congo's leadership in organizing African countries to work together for common aims.

PORTRAITS OF THE NATIONS SERIES

THE LAND AND PEOPLE OF AFGHANISTAN
THE LAND AND PEOPLE OF ALGERIA
THE LAND AND PEOPLE OF ARGENTINA
THE LAND AND PEOPLE OF AUSTRALIA
THE LAND AND PEOPLE OF AUSTRIA
THE LAND AND PEOPLE OF THE BALKANS
THE LAND AND PEOPLE OF BELGIUM
THE LAND AND PEOPLE OF BRAZIL
THE LAND AND PEOPLE OF BURMA
THE LAND AND PEOPLE OF CANADA
THE LAND AND PEOPLE OF CENTRAL AMERICA
THE LAND AND PEOPLE OF CEYLON
THE LAND AND PEOPLE OF CHILE
THE LAND AND PEOPLE OF CHINA
THE LAND AND PEOPLE OF COLOMBIA
THE LAND AND PEOPLE OF THE CONGO
THE LAND AND PEOPLE OF CZECHOSLOVAKIA
THE LAND AND PEOPLE OF DENMARK
THE LAND AND PEOPLE OF EGYPT
THE LAND AND PEOPLE OF ENGLAND
THE LAND AND PEOPLE OF ETHIOPIA
THE LAND AND PEOPLE OF FINLAND
THE LAND AND PEOPLE OF FRANCE
THE LAND AND PEOPLE OF GERMANY
THE LAND AND PEOPLE OF GHANA
THE LAND AND PEOPLE OF GREECE
THE LAND AND PEOPLE OF THE GUIANAS
THE LAND AND PEOPLE OF HOLLAND
THE LAND AND PEOPLE OF HUNGARY
THE LAND AND PEOPLE OF ICELAND
THE LAND AND PEOPLE OF INDIA
THE LAND AND PEOPLE OF INDONESIA
THE LAND AND PEOPLE OF IRAN
THE LAND AND PEOPLE OF IRAQ
THE LAND AND PEOPLE OF IRELAND
THE LAND AND PEOPLE OF ISRAEL
THE LAND AND PEOPLE OF ITALY
THE LAND AND PEOPLE OF JAPAN
THE LAND AND PEOPLE OF JORDAN
THE LAND AND PEOPLE OF KENYA
THE LAND AND PEOPLE OF KOREA
THE LAND AND PEOPLE OF LEBANON
THE LAND AND PEOPLE OF LIBERIA
THE LAND AND PEOPLE OF LIBYA
THE LAND AND PEOPLE OF MALAYSIA
THE LAND AND PEOPLE OF MEXICO
THE LAND AND PEOPLE OF MOROCCO
THE LAND AND PEOPLE OF NEW ZEALAND
THE LAND AND PEOPLE OF NIGERIA
THE LAND AND PEOPLE OF NORWAY
THE LAND AND PEOPLE OF PAKISTAN
THE LAND AND PEOPLE OF PERU
THE LAND AND PEOPLE OF THE PHILIPPINES
THE LAND AND PEOPLE OF POLAND
THE LAND AND PEOPLE OF PORTUGAL
THE LAND AND PEOPLE OF RHODESIA
THE LAND AND PEOPLE OF ROMANIA
THE LAND AND PEOPLE OF RUSSIA
THE LAND AND PEOPLE OF SCOTLAND
THE LAND AND PEOPLE OF SOUTH AFRICA
THE LAND AND PEOPLE OF SPAIN
THE LAND AND PEOPLE OF SWEDEN
THE LAND AND PEOPLE OF SWITZERLAND
THE LAND AND PEOPLE OF SYRIA
THE LAND AND PEOPLE OF TANGANYIKA
THE LAND AND PEOPLE OF THAILAND
THE LAND AND PEOPLE OF TUNISIA
THE LAND AND PEOPLE OF TURKEY
THE LAND AND PEOPLE OF URUGUAY
THE LAND AND PEOPLE OF VENEZUELA
THE LAND AND PEOPLE OF THE WEST INDIES

Also in the same format

THE ISLANDS OF HAWAII   THE ISLAND OF PUERTO RICO

The Land and People of the
CONGO

by Louise Crane

PORTRAITS OF THE NATIONS SERIES

J. B. LIPPINCOTT COMPANY
Philadelphia   New York

Acknowledgments

Grateful acknowledgment is made to the following: Dr. David McLean of St. Andrews College, Laurinburg, N.C. for Lulua proverbs and prayers quoted in Chapter 9; to *Présence Africaine* for permission to translate and print poems of Étienne Tshinday Lukumbi (from *Marche, Pays des Espoirs*)

Special acknowledgment is made to Ambassador Théodor Idzumbuir and Mlle. Philomène Makolu of the Congo UN Mission, and many Congolese friends who helped with contributions to and critical comments on the manuscript for this book; such acknowledgment by no means implies their full endorsement of all points of judgment, for which I assume full responsibility.

The author wishes to thank the following for the photographs which appear in this book: Bibliotheque Nationale du Congo, page 88; Mary Bobb, page 89; Congopresse, J. Makula, p. 44 and C. Lamote, p. 67; Republique Democratique du Congo Information Service, pages 25, 92, 95, 108, 109, 127 (top); United Nations, pages 12, 51, 64, 73, 127 (bottom); and Zaire, pages 14, 19, 20, 46, 50, 61, 65, 70, 78, 83, 98, 100, 106, 111, 113, 115, 119, 122, 130, 133, 135, 137.

Copyright © 1971 by Louise Crane
All Rights Reserved
Printed in the United States of America
Library of Congress Catalog Card Number 79-141447
Second Printing
Map by Donald T. Pitcher
ISBN-0-397-31172-9 Trade Ed.
ISBN-0-397-31173-7 LLB Ed.

TO HANK CRANE

Contents

1	*Mbote, Muoyo Webe, Bonjour, Jambo!*	11
2	Kongo Kings	21
3	Adventurers in the "Heart of Darkness"	28
4	Belgian Kings	33
5	*Dipanda*	38
6	From *Dipanda* to Operation Shirtsleeves	48
7	The Government of the Republic	55
8	The People	63
9	Religion	72
10	Education and Health	86
11	Diamonds in the Dirt	94
12	Language and Communication	103
13	Art and Music	110
14	Liberation of Women and Youth	118
15	Life in the Country, Life in the Town	126
16	"Bring Me the Head and Feet with Which I Can March Forward!"	132
	Index	138

The Land and People of the
CONGO

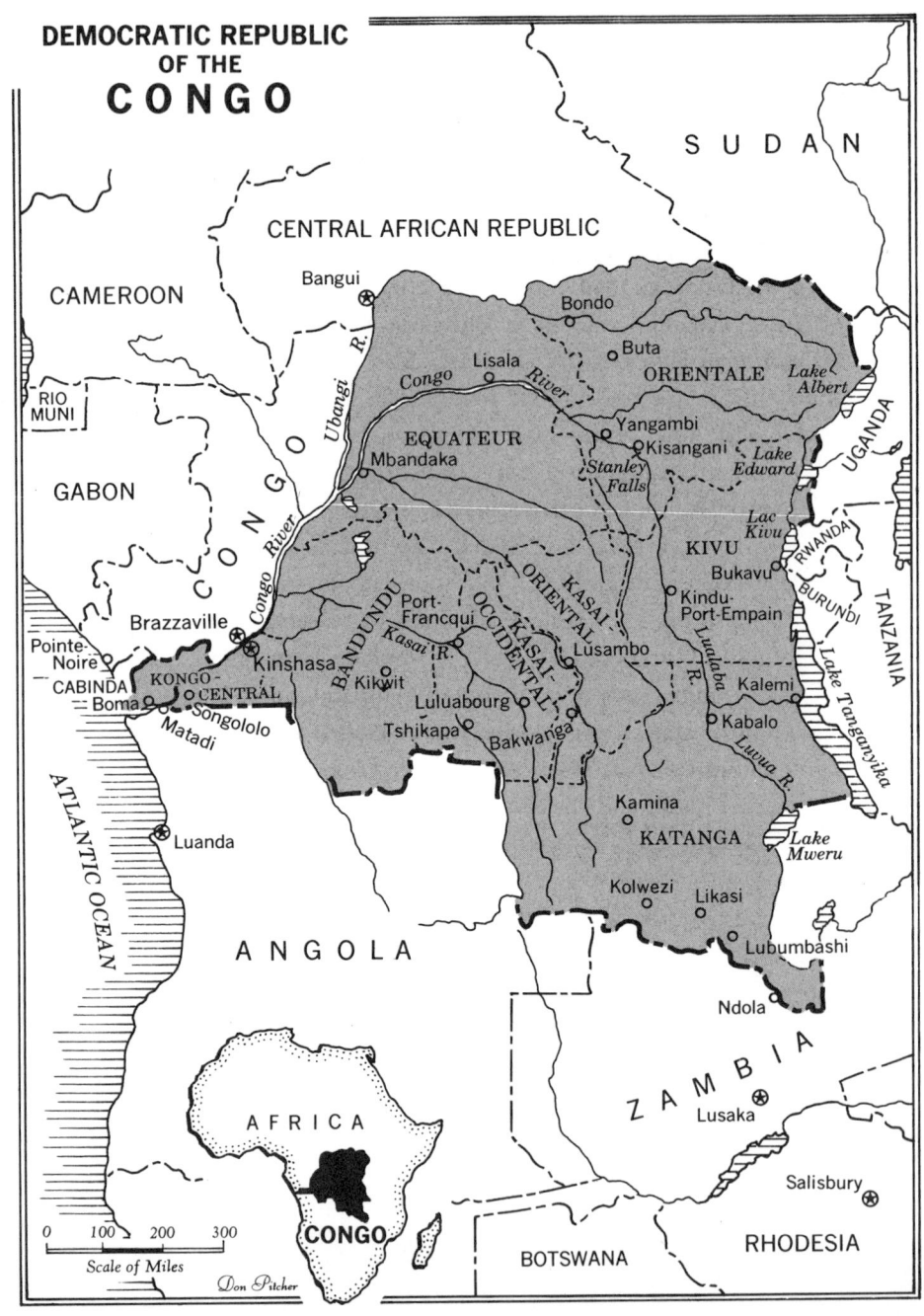

1

Mbote, Muoyo Webe, Bonjour, Jambo!

Your welcome at Njili, one of Africa's largest airports, may be in Lingala, Tshiluba, French, perhaps Swahili or Kikongo, but you can be *sure* of one thing: You have just landed in one of the most exciting countries on the continent, the Democratic Republic of the Congo.

Should you arrive at night, you will be dazzled immediately by the brilliantly lighted skyline of Kinshasa, capital of the Congo and—with a population of one-and-a-half million—the third-largest French-speaking city in the world. Whirring along Avenue Patrice Lumumba with hundreds of taxis and buses carrying travelers from all over the world, you soon arrive in the heart of the capital, and—if you are a newcomer—you will be overwhelmed with the extraordinary beauty of this African city. There are tall, impressive white buildings, magnificent villas, tree-lined streets, Boulevard du 30 Juin reminiscent of the Champs Elysees with its sidewalk cafes, chic and elegant people strolling about. Signs of the jet age are everywhere. There are diesel engines purring, shrill whistles from the river traffic, screeching brakes, radio and television blaring from lighted windows. You would certainly be impressed, but per-

Congo River scene

haps also somewhat disappointed, for possibly you were expecting the exotic tropical jungle described by Joseph Conrad in *Heart of Darkness,* or something more picturesquely African, such as a Pygmy as he is pictured by one of the modern-day adventurers or moviemakers? The Congo River, so romantically described by poets and writers, is choked with dirty barges and diesel-run boats; steel docks and cranes line the shores.

Don't go away! Congo won't disappoint you. It still has all the adventure, mystery, and beauty described by the poets. Much of the old traditional life is still here, but it is mixed with new things, for Congo, too, must move forward. If you look hard enough you will see canoes here and there on the river or tied up at some shady spot on the bank, only a few feet away from an embassy villa flanked with palms and scarlet- and blue-flowered trees. Echoes of the golden age of the Kingdom of Kongo, thriving before the discovery of America, will sound in surprising places.

Variations of modern city life, on a smaller scale, can be found elsewhere in Congo: Kisangani in Orientale Province, Luluabourg in Kasai Occidental, or Lubumbashi in the southeastern area of Katanga Province. The old Congo is here also in the small villages scattered through more than 900,000 square miles of country (one-third the size of the United States) in which people are living the simple way of their ancestors, observing the old tribal rites and customs. Even in the cities it does not take long to find the old Congo hovering close. A traditional wail frequently breaks the European formality of the funeral cortege for a government official. At the outdoor market men, women, and children of every nationality, plunged together in an overpowering aroma of manioc roots, palm oil, dried meats, and fish, yell at each other in traditional African bargaining. A Kinshasa teen-ager in search of his identity may make a pilgrimage to his ancestral village in Equateur Province to study folklore. The Congo government officials wear caps of imitation leopard skin, the leopard being the traditional symbol of power and authority. The *Ordre du Léopard* (Order of the Leopard) is the highest Congolese honor that can be bestowed on a person.

Everywhere there are reminders of people involved in the Congo's past. Stanley Pool, which separates Kinshasa from Brazzaville, capital of the former French Congo, bears the name of the British-American explorer who came to Africa in 1871 to search for David Livingstone and returned to claim the Congo for the Belgian king, Leopold II. On top of Mont Stanley, overlooking the Congo River, a statue of the explorer surveys the country. Behind it are three figures, each symbolizing a typical Congolese of Stanley's day: a hunter, a fisherman, and a farmer. (Each of these three figures stands over six feet tall—said to be the average size of the Congolese at that time—while the figure of Stanley is much shorter.) Mont Stanley is also the site of the presidential palace and of the O.A.U. center, a group of forty-two individual pavilions for the nations belonging to the Organization of African Unity.

Kinshasa was known as Léopoldville after the Belgian king who first took over the Congo, but it changed to the original African name several years after the country became independent of Belgian rule, on June 30, 1960. Boulevard du 30 Juin recalls the birthdate of the Democratic Republic of the Congo, as does the

OAU Center on top of Mont Stanley

avenue named for Patrice Lumumba, the Congolese leader so deeply involved in its beginning. As a symbol of the universal struggle for freedom, the name Lumumba has been given to children, streets, and institutions all over the world.

Geographically, as in all other respects, the Congo presents many contrasts, from deep, dark jungles and rain forests to snow-capped mountains. It is one of the few African countries that has natural physical boundaries, all situated around the central basin of the Congo River, which was once an inland sea. In the north there is a savannah region, hot and humid, crossed by the equator at the upper third of the country. A chain of mountains called the Crystal Mountains runs west of the basin, bordering the French Congo (known as the People's Republic of Congo since it, too, became independent in 1960) and extending to the Portuguese colony of Angola. (Both Congos and Angola share the history of the ancient Kingdom of Kongo discovered by the Portuguese in 1482.) In the south, the basin is rimmed again by plains and the Katanga highlands bordering on Zambia. The eastern lake region is the most scenic and attractive, with its temperate climate. Here is the Great Rift Valley, 869 miles long and 25 miles wide. Each of its large lakes is shared with another country: Lake Albert with Uganda; Lake Kivu with Rwanda; the very long Lake Tanganyika with three countries—Burundi, Tanzania, and Zambia. Zambia also shares the shores of Lake Mweru on the southeast end, as well as the source of the Congo River, the Zambezi. David Livingstone discovered this origin of the Congo River, rather by accident, in 1867. Across the Rift Valley lies a chain of volcanic mountains, some of which are still active. These mountains, the Virunga, rise as high as 15,000 feet and form the end of the Congo-Nile divide; the Nile watershed is on the north, the Congo watershed, south. North of the Virunga is an even higher chain of mountains, the

Ruwenzori, rising to nearly 17,000 feet and perpetually covered with snow and ice. These mountains appeared as "The Mountains of the Moon" on a map drawn by Ptolemy, the second-century A.D. astronomer and geographer of Alexandria.

The pleasant climate, breathtaking beauty, and fascinating wildlife make the eastern lake region a favorite destination for tourists. Albert National Park, a wildlife sanctuary in the Kivu area, covering over 3,000 miles of glaciers, forests, plains, volcanoes, and rivers, offers firsthand observation of the animals that are native to the Congo: gorillas, elephants, leopards, lions, hippopotamuses, crocodiles, and many more. The world's tallest people, the seven-foot Watusi, and the shortest, the four-foot Pygmies, also live in this area.

There are two other national parks of considerable size, Upemba and Garamba, and many smaller game reserves. Tourist attractions in other parts of the Congo include many falls and cascades: Tshopo Falls at Kisangani, Lualaba and Johnson falls in Katanga; the mysterious grottoes of Thysville; the Mayumbe forest; the garden of Frère Gillet at Kisantu; the botanical gardens of Eala on the equator; the beaches of Moanda; the valley of the Ruzizi; and the incredible Lake Fua in Kasai.

The climate and seasons vary in these regions of the Congo according to their relation to the equator. Except for the eastern highlands, the climate is generally hot and humid, averaging about 77 degrees Fahrenheit, ranging from 60 to 100 degrees Fahrenheit at the equator. There are rainy and dry seasons. On the north side of the equator the rainy season generally lasts from April through October; the dry season starting in November is relatively cool. For the areas south of the equator the time for rainy and dry seasons is reversed. Sometimes there are two short dry seasons and two short wet or rainy seasons, often with little temperature change.

For many people in the Congo, measurement of time and season is not a matter of clocks and calendars, but rather of observing the movements of the sun and moon or the living patterns of animals and birds. An old Lulua proverb puts it this way: "If you disagree with the bat and the rooster, how are you going to tell time?"

Unfortunately, bats and roosters often cannot be heard above the noise of city traffic, so the people in Lubumbashi and Kinshasa have had to buy clocks. This is only one of thousands of ways the Congo has had to change since it emerged into the modern world.

Although many people elsewhere in the world have become aware of this country only recently, products of the Congo have for many years made their way into homes all over the world. The ivory keys of your piano, the small diamonds used in the inner parts of your watch or for your record player needle, copper pots in your kitchen, Palmolive soap in your bathroom, or perhaps your morning coffee—all might have had their origin in the Congo.

The Congo ranks high as supplier of many of the world's natural resources. It is the world's largest producer of industrial diamonds, the second-largest supplier of gem stones. Union Minière du Haut Katanga once ranked fourth in the world's copper production; under the new, post-independence regime of Gecomin, a mining syndicate, these mines are still an important source of copper. The Katanga area also ranked recently as fifteenth in supply of the world's gold. Over half of the free world's supply of two other important minerals—uranium and cobalt—comes from Congo. Tin, zinc, and manganese are available here in large quantity. Other principal resources of this country are: palm products, coffee, rubber, cotton, ivory, and copal. Congo controls half of Africa's share of potential hydroelectric resources and 13 percent of the world total; most of these reserves are at Inga, twenty-five miles above Matadi.

Not only is Congo rich in the resources of its land, but its people are among the most artistic in the world. Congo sculpture has fascinated art connoisseurs for hundreds of years and appears now in museums all over the world; it has been a source of inspiration to many contemporary artists. The *Missa Luba,* a Congolese mass originating at Luluabourg in the Kasai area, has provided theme music for several internationally known movies. Jazz from Congo is not only played all over Africa, but has worldwide popularity.

Over two hundred identifiable tribes inhabit the Congo in the following major groupings and approximate percentages: Bantu, 70 percent; Sudanese, 20 percent; Pygmy, 7 percent; Nilotics and Hamitics, 3 percent. The official language of the country is that introduced by the Belgian colonialists, that is, French, though most Congolese speak several Bantu dialects. Lingala is generally accepted as the language of the ANC, the Congo army. Other major dialects are Kingwana (a form of Swahili), Tshiluba, and Kikongo.

Over sixty thousand foreigners are included in the population of of the Congo, which has grown from 13 million in 1960 to an estimated 19 million ten years later. The foreigners include members of other African countries, Europeans, Americans, and Asiatics.

Allow plenty of time for your visit to Congo. Travel in Africa is generally unpredictable, though in many respects it is quickly catching up to Europe and America. Kinshasa is on the main route of international flights and land routes are being constantly expanded. Within the country itself Air Congo flies to all major cities and some smaller airlines and private planes cover more remote posts. Roads, railways, and air service are still not adequate for this vast country, over four times the size of France, but massive plans are underway to improve them. One of the slower but more picturesque ways to get around is via the Congo River, stretching

Post office at Kinshasa

out for 3,000 miles into all corners of the country. Passenger boats of Otraco, Congo's major shipping company, make regular runs over quite a bit of it.

The Congo is not built for 21-day package tours. In Kinshasa alone you could race around at top-speed day and night for several weeks and only begin to cover the sights in and around the capital: Mont Stanley, the Beaux Arts Museum, Lovanium University, the Kimbanguist cathedral, the Ivory Market, the model fishing village Kinkole, and N'sele, which is President Mobutu's farm project, to name only a few. And Kinshasa is certainly not all of Congo. There are other cities worth visiting, such as Lubumbashi, Kisangani, and Matadi, but more time should be allowed for the natural wonders. The African Travel Bureau in Goma, which has branches also in Kinshasa and Lubumbashi, will be happy to arrange a tour through Albert National Park, an excursion up the volcanic mountain, or a five-hour ride across beautiful Lake Kivu to Bukavu. Or you might take a ride across the rapids with Wagenia fishermen at Stanley Falls, a trip through the mines at Mbuji-Mayi or Lubumbashi. Accomodations vary from a deluxe suite at the new Intercontinental Hotel in Kinshasa to the smaller, but delightfully comfortable Hotel des Grands Lacs overlooking Lake Kivu (at Goma), to simple grass-thatched rest houses in the parks or the villages. As in all foreign travel, it would make your trip much more meaningful if you could speak directly to some of the local inhabitants—a brushup on French is therefore most advisable.

The journey from Kisangani to Boma, which took Stanley eight months in 1877, can now be made within a few hours by air. Nevertheless it takes a lot of time to understand even a little of the many forces and events that have shaped the modern Democratic Republic of the Congo.

Visit of Apollo 11 *astronauts to Kinshasa, October 1969. (Crowds waiting outside U.S.I.S. Center)*

2

Kongo Kings

In 1482 a Portuguese sailor with mixed-up ideas of geography was sailing along the west coast of Africa looking for the basin of the Nile. Instead, Diego Cão stumbled into the mouth of another great river, called "Nzadi" or "big water" by the local inhabitants. The Portuguese promptly changed "Nzadi" to "Zaire," which was easier for them to pronounce, but many years later the river was given an African name, Congo, as it is known today. The Portuguese word, however, is not forgotten: "Zaire" is the name of the largest currency denomination in modern Congo and is equivalent to about two U.S. dollars; it is the title of one of the most popular weekly journals and is also the name of a national order. The *Ordre du Zaire* was conferred on André Watts, a young American pianist of African descent, when President Mobutu heard him perform at a special White House concert; this was during the Congolese President's official visit to the United States in August, 1970.

The name "Congo" originated from the Kingdom of the Kongo which Diego Cão found flourishing when he arrived. This ancient kingdom, dating back to at least the middle of the fourteenth century, was made up largely of the Bakongo people. Its original domain and descendants are now parts of three modern countries:

the Portuguese colony of Angola, the People's Republic of Congo,[1] and the Democratic Republic of the Congo[1].

The Portuguese and the Africans were impressed with each other and things started out friendly enough. At the Kongo capital, Mbanza Kongo, the foreigners were welcomed by thousands of brilliantly painted warriors armed with bows and arrows, wearing magnificent headdresses of red parrot feathers, playing ivory trumpets, iron double-bells, and violalike musical instruments, and of course the royal drums. In Lisbon the ambassador of the Mani-Kongo (title of the King of Kongo) was received with similar fanfare. African and European monarchs addressed each other warmly as "most powerful and excellent king . . . king my brother." Soon, however, the exchange became unequal. Few of the Portuguese coming to Africa bothered to learn the local language or find out about the customs and religious beliefs of the people whose guests they were; instead they started teaching the Bakongo to do things in their way. They even gave the capital a new name, São Salvador. The people of Kongo did not object seriously to this, for they were impressed with the foreign goods, especially the firearms, and thought perhaps belief in the foreign God might give them additional power against their own enemies. Kings and noblemen accepted baptism, changed their names to "Christian" ones, and requested the Portuguese to send more missionaries, technicians, and teachers into their land. The reign of the second Christian king, Alfonso I—whose original name was Nzinga Mbemba—was the period of greatest communication between Portugal and the Kongo, but it ended in tragedy and disillusionment. So eager was this monarch for learning that it was said of him: "He does nothing but

---

[1] Unless otherwise indicated, hereafter "Congo" will refer to the modern Democratic Republic of the Congo.

study . . . he falls asleep over his books, forgets the time to dine." When Alfonso I visited the king in Lisbon or the Pope in Rome he could speak to them in their own languages. Furthermore he wanted this enlightenment for as many of his African subjects as possible and started sending young men to Europe for study. One of these, Dom Henrique, became the first Catholic bishop in the Kongo in 1518. However by 1539 Alfonso was writing a letter to the Portuguese king to complain about the fate of twenty young students sent to Lisbon some sixteen years earlier. Ten of these had been taken as slaves on the way to Portugal, and nothing had been heard from any of the others.

By this time the Christianizing mission of Portugal had joined hands with the slavery movement and was aiding the exploitation of the Africans. Both sides were to blame, foreigners and Africans. Some of the foreigners had started out with real desire to help, but others had rushed to the Kongo mainly to help themselves, spurred by rumors of "solid mountains of silver" and an "isle of silver." Both rumors were misleading: the "Isle of Silver" was the name given by the Bakongo to Loanda, an island full of baby cowrie shells known as "nzimbu." "Nzimbu" were used for money by the people of the Kongo: a chicken could be bought with fifty nzimbu, a goat for three hundred, and a necklace or bracelet of nzimbu was considered priceless. Gold or silver, by comparison, were of little value—to the Bakongo. But since the Portuguese used the word meaning "silver" for money, they went along with that, too. It was just too bad if the ignorant white people did not understand that their "silver island" really meant an island full of Kongo money, nzimbu.

In spite of their disappointment in not finding great quantities of gold and silver, the Portuguese did discover plenty to fill their pockets: such rare treasures as ivory, skins, copper, and the fine raffia cloth woven by the people of the region. As the foreigners and Africans alike accumulated wealth, trading grew more and more elaborate and greedy, finally resulting in the selling of human beings.

Slavery had been practiced before this by Africans and non-Africans, but in an entirely different way. Traditionally, captives of war, criminals or very often peasants of lower class were required to perform military service, household work, or to provide certain services, such as fishing or forging, without pay. Such wageless workers, slaves, were not outcasts. They often lived with their masters, sometimes marrying the masters' daughters, and were recognized members of the community. They could even earn back their freedom. But the slavery introduced with the discovery of the Americas was quite a different kind. The new lands needed a vast amount of manpower that could not be supplied by volunteers. The Africans who were imported to work in America were taken against their will, stripped of all individual rights and privileges, chained and branded like cattle. The business of selling slaves for forced labor became highly profitable, both for the Africans who sold them, and for the foreigners who bought and sold them to overseas owners. At first, captives of war or other undesirable citizens of the Kongo were used for trade, but the demand soon became so great that people sold members of their own family in order to themselves enjoy the privileges of modernization. One nobleman in São Salvador paid an annual tuition fee of several slaves to keep his sons in school. By the end of the first century of European occupation, over half a million slaves—many of them the elite, of noble families—had been taken out of the Kongo. A conservative estimate of 1836 put the number of slaves exported from the Congo region by that time at over 5 million, more than the present population of Angola.

The Christian Mani-Kongo, Alfonso I, was anxious to modernize his country and so had himself participated at first in the slave business. But when members of his own family and some of the very educated young men he counted on were snatched away as slaves, he tried to put a stop to it. By then it was too late.

Following the death of Alfonso I in 1561, the Kingdom of the Kongo declined rapidly, as foreigners competed with each other to exploit the land and the people, and rival tribes fought for power. In 1575 Portugal made an outright conquest of the southern region, naming it Angola for one of the local kings, Ngola; this area has remained under Portuguese rule to this day. In the middle of the nineteenth century the rest of the kingdom was divided between

Lualaba Falls, Katanga

France and Belgium, but by that time the kingdom itself was little more than a memory. However, the Bakongo people, though separated into three countries, are still very mindful of their roots and are often influential in political and government decisions.

Other kingdoms, too, flourished in Congo in ancient times, though we can only mention them here. There is good evidence that the southeastern part of modern Congo, Katanga, was probably the early home of Bantu-speaking people over two thousand years ago. The use of iron had been known among the Bantu since some fifty years before the birth of Christ and spread from the Congo area to the south and east. During the first thousand years A.D., metal-using states developed from scattered communities, organizing into states with kings and central governments. One of the strongest of these was the Luba empire, established in 1400 with its founding hero, Kongolo, beginning a tradition of royal successors known as "balopwe"[1]. In 1600 a Luba "mulopwe"[1] by the name of Kibinda Ilunga founded a new state among the Lunda by marrying a local queen; successors to the Lunda throne carried the traditional title, "Mwata Yamvo," and have continued political influence down to modern times. Moise Tshombe, Prime Minister of the Congo from 1964 to 1965, was a son-in-law of the Mwata Yamvo in Katanga.

Another kingdom flourished briefly in the latter nineteenth century, headed by a young man of royal descent named Msiri. Msiri established an important trade center in the upper Katanga, dealing in ivory, copper, salt, iron, and slaves, and guarded by an army of ten thousand soldiers equipped with firearms. After he was shot down by a Belgian lieutenant in 1891, Msiri's empire virtually vanished, but his descendants continue to have political prestige.

---

[1] "balopwe," plural; "mulopwe," singular.

The Bakuba or Bushongo kingdom in the West Kasai province of modern Congo, has preserved its artistic and ritual traditions amazingly intact down to modern times, though it has kept somewhat aloof from national politics. "Lukenge" is the name given to the successors to the Bakuba throne, who date back to the fifth century A.D. For many years this region has fascinated moviemakers, art connoisseurs, and general sightseers. Anyone who has a command of the language and the time to listen can learn a great deal of Africa's past through the oral recitations at King Lukenge's court. Some years ago a Belgian by the name of Torday had been listening for many hours to Bushongo elders droning on about their past. They had come to the ninety-eighth chief when one of them made a remark that caused Torday to jump out of his seat. Nothing special had happened during Bo Kama Bomanchala's reign, the old man said casually, except for one day when the "sun went out" and there was absolute darkness for a while. Hearing this, the Belgian went wild with excitement, for he realized that this could refer to nothing else than the one and only total sun eclipse visible in the Bushongo area during the seventeenth and eighteenth centuries; this had occurred in March, 1680. Now Torday was certain that Bo Kama Bomanchala had reigned at the time of the sun eclipse, in 1680, and he could fit all the other events described by the Bushongo elder into definite dates.

3

Adventurers in the "Heart of Darkness"

By the beginning of the nineteenth century many outsiders drifted into the Congo from all directions. Two Portuguese traders, called "pombeiros," traveling east from Angola in 1806, made a visit to one of the Kazembe, sub-chiefs of the Mwata Yamvo, and were not only impressed with his splendid appearance, but noted in their diary that "green stones are found in the earth named catanga." This, of course, was evidence of the large copper deposits that were to make Katanga famous in later years.

Arab slave traders, Swahili-speaking mulattoes from the east coast, had started caravans into East Africa as early as 1820, and by 1840 they were established in the eastern part of Congo. David Livingstone, Henry Stanley, and other European explorers had to secure the cooperation of the Arabs for safe conduct through this area. The most powerful trader, Tippo Tip, was made a governor of a large province for a while, after Leopold II had taken over the Congo.

During the early 1800's there were several British expeditions: one headed by Captain Tuckey and sponsored by the Royal Geographical Society of London attempted to go up the Congo

River from the west coast. Soon after reaching Matadi, they were stopped by the rapids of Yellela Falls at Isingila (later dubbed "Tuckey's Farthest" by Stanley); search for a land route ended in death by fever of most of the crew, including Captain Tuckey. Two other Englishmen, Sir Richard Burton and John Hanning Speke, started from the east coast in search of the Nile source and landed at Lake Tanganyika in 1858, neither one of them realizing they had come to the source of the Congo. Another Englishman, Sir Samuel Baker, named a lake which he found on the northeast border of Congo, between Congo and Uganda, Lake Albert, after the husband of Queen Victoria.

Other explorers came from all over Europe: Greece, Italy, Hungary, Germany, and so on. One of the German explorers was George Augustus Schweinfurth, who discovered and wrote about the Pygmies.

The Nile continued to fascinate explorers more than the Congo. The Scottish missionary-explorer, David Livingstone, also came looking for the source of the Nile, and discovered two lakes—Lake Mweru and Lake Bangwelu—which proved to be the headwaters of the Congo as well as of another important African river, the Zambezi. Livingstone's health broke down soon after this and he lost touch with the outside world. When there had been no direct word from him for five years, his friends in Europe and America got worried. Henry Morton Stanley, a British-born reporter who had become an American citizen and fought on both sides of the Civil War, was sent to Africa to look for Livingstone; his trip was financed by the American paper for which he worked, *The New York Herald*.

"Dr. Livingstone, I presume?" said Stanley to the famous missionary as he met him at last on the shores of Lake Tanganyika on November 10, 1871. Though grateful for the supplies brought by the American caravan, Livingstone preferred to remain with his African friends. He died some months later near Lake Bangwela, in modern Zambia, while Stanley returned to write *How I Found Livingstone.* On a later expedition, in 1874, financed this time by both *The New York Herald* and the *London Daily Telegraph,* Stanley retraced the steps of Livingstone and earlier explorers along Lake Tanganyika and the Lulualaba River (a tributary of the Congo), then made some discoveries of his own. Among them was Stanley Falls at the Wagenia fishing villages across from the modern city of Kisangani (formerly called Stanleyville). Following the Congo River, often dodging spears and arrows, Stanley and his men reached a wide "pool" in the river on March 12, 1877, and heard a rumble of falls beyond it. With no qualms at all about leaving his name on yet another site, the British-American explorer accepted the title of "Stanley Pool" for this place and proceeded on to the mouth of the river. This part of the trip had to be done on foot, around the rapids, with supreme effort, but finally in August, 1877, the bedraggled group of 115 men, women, and children reached Boma at the mouth of the Congo River. Stanley's story of this expedition, *Through the Dark Continent,* was immediately a bestseller, for it was an exciting adventure story. Though his writing aroused international interest in the injustices of the slave trade in Africa, Stanley was himself an egotistical, ambitious man who sometimes used the Congolese to gain his own goals. When they did not see things his way he called them ignorant savages. However, Stanley's name remains prominently displayed throughout the Congo, as does that of Leopold II, the ambitious king with whom he helped exploit the prize country. For, typically tolerant and realistic, the Congolese people also recognize the positive contributions made by these two men.

When King Leopold II of Belgium, a first cousin of Queen Vic-

Statues on Mont Stanley: Stanley, a Congolese hunter, fisherman, and a farmer (See description, pages 13-14)

toria of England, heard of Stanley's successful expedition, he immediately sent representatives to see him. At that time, when all the European powers were scrambling for foreign possessions, Belgium had no colony; to Leopold the Congo sounded like an ideal prize. But Stanley gave first choice to his mother country, England. The queen, unimpressed by his boasts of tremendous wealth in Congo—copper, gold, palm oil, and valuable woods—turned him down. So, after Queen Victoria's rejection, Stanley accepted Leopold's invitation to visit him in Belgium.

4

Belgian Kings

For some time before Stanley's successful mission to the Congo, Leopold II, second king of Belgium and honorary president of the International African Association—which he had himself originated—had been looking for some way to get a foothold in Africa. Though his declared aim was to abolish the slave trade and open the continent to international trade, he was most concerned about his own country's prestige. Congo offered the perfect opportunity.

Following a magnificent reception at the Belgian court in June, 1878, Stanley consented to join Leopold II in a business enterprise entitled "Study of the Upper Congo." Within four years a road had been built to bypass the rapids between Matadi and Stanley Pool, thirty posts had been established through the country, and treaties signed with local chiefs. The French were also negotiating with chiefs along the Congo River; a French explorer, Savorgnan de Brazza, discovered Stanley Pool shortly after the British-American expedition had been there. Leopold tried to engage him also, but he remained loyal to his own country. After the Congo territory was divided between Belgium and France, the capitals of the two countries faced each other across the river at Stanley Pool: Brazzaville on the French side, Léopoldville (Kinshasa) on the Belgian side.

Before this, however, there was a general scramble among all the European nations for possession of Africa. At a conference called in 1885 at Berlin to settle claims, King Leopold II got official recognition for his personal ownership of the Congo Free State. The Belgian Government itself at that time was skeptical of the possibilities of the Congo and was content to let the king keep it as his private commercial enterprise rather than accept responsibility for it as a Belgian colony.

In May, 1885, Leopold set his superb organizing ability and business skills to developing the Congo Free State into a profitable venture. The rich mineral area of Katanga was given an organization of its own, Compagnie du Katanga, which later played a very important role in the economic and political life of Congo. Leopold tried to establish a monopoly on the two most important products of that time, ivory and rubber, but the free trade guarantees of the Act of Berlin forced him to make a compromise. He tried to fight his biggest competitors in the ivory trade, the Arabs, under the guise of "anti-slavery" moves, but was often forced to make deals with them instead.

A system of taxation enforced by state agents increased the exportation of rubber from eighty-two metric tons in 1891 to 6,000 metric tons in 1901, but the ruthlessness and cruelty of Leopold's methods drew international protest. While piously proclaiming to end the barbarism of slavery, Leopold and his representatives stopped at nothing to gain their ends: those who fought the system or refused to bring in their quotas were maimed, many massacred. In Joseph Conrad's novel, *Heart of Darkness,* which was based on this period in the Congo, the trader Kurtz reflects many of the characteristics of Leopold and his agents. In 1904 the Congo Reform Association, alarmed by reports of the atrocities which had come from Protestant missionaries, launched an investigation.

Though King Leopold himself spent large sums in public relations and lobbying activities—some involving the United States—and appeared to cooperate with the investigations, the Congo Free State was finally removed from his personal domain in 1908 and annexed to Belgium as a colony. The next year Leopold died.

As a Belgian colony, the Congo was more directly involved with the Brussels Government, but it continued up to independence in 1960 to have a special relation to each of the three kings who succeeded Leopold II: Albert, Leopold III, and Baudouin. The Belgian Minister for the Colonies was a member of the king's cabinet in Brussels and the colony was headed by a Belgian Governor-General in the capital of Leopoldville. Belgian vice-governors, provincial governors, territorial administrators, tax collectors, and state officers of various sorts represented the administration throughout the colony. There was an attempt to include local chiefs in the administrative system, but it was only partially successful because always the system was Belgian, not African. Chiefs were arbitrarily appointed or dismissed by the administration according to their "efficiency."

For a long time the white men occupying Africa had justified their dominating the "natives" with the assumption that the black inhabitants were inferior in intelligence and maturity and that true "civilization" could come only from Europe. One of the ablest and most benevolent of the Belgian colonial administrators, Governor General Pierre Ryckmans, summed up the general attitude in his famous 1946 farewell address, *"Dominer pour Servir"* (Dominate to Serve):

> "If I were to leave you a last message, I would tell you that the function of the State is to make and to safeguard man's happiness, that a country's prosperity is the pros-

perity of the mass of its inhabitants and that Belgium shall have completed her colonial task when our natives live happily under the shadow of our flag."

Some ten years later the governor's son, André Ryckmans, referring to a widely publicized proclamation of Belgian-Congolese cooperation known as the Belgo-Congolese Community, made this remark:

"As for the Belgo-Congolese Community, I sincerely wonder if there is a single African who believes in it; the Africans are psychologists enough to recognize the enormous ingredient of hypocrisy there is in the present declarations . . . there is nothing so ridiculous as an all-purpose slogan."

Throughout the Belgian occupation of Congo, the official policy was that the welfare of the Congolese came first; a Standing Commission for the Protection of Natives had been written into the colonial charter. The Belgians worked diligently to provide what they considered ideal goals for each Congolese: money in the pocket, a job, education and medical care, church, and perhaps some technical training. By the time they turned over the Government to the Congolese in 1960, over 40 percent of the population was literate and the health program was one of the best in Africa. The general living standard was high in comparison to that of other African countries, many Congolese having their own bank accounts. For everyone—Congolese and Belgians—benefited from the increased production and profits from exports.

But the cost of economic prosperity was high for the Congolese. Thousands were uprooted from their ancestral homes and moved into crowded mining communities to supply the manpower needed by the large European companies. It became "good business" to compensate these displaced people with free housing for their families, food, clothing, medical care, and schools. It was a fairly comfortable slavery but it still was slavery, for even their leisure time was regulated for them, and they were told how to spend their money.

The same pattern existed in the Catholic and Protestant missions, which often served as agents of colonialism: The "natives" were treated well, but a great part of their lives was ordered by the white people. As one Congolese remarked, "You don't realize you are a slave until you try to be different."

All over the Congo, many of the old African values and systems were broken down, often repudiated by Congolese who were very anxious to become modern, but what replaced them was a confusing structure mainly imposed by white men with little respect for African personality and thinking.

The pageantry of the kings continued: King Albert and his Queen Elizabeth made an official visit in 1928 to dedicate the Congo division of the Cape to Cairo railroad, and waved to cheering throngs at each whistle stop along the jungle-lined route. Prince Leopold followed soon after, then made a later visit when he was crowned Leopold III. Congolese sang 'La Brabançonne" lustily and reverently saluted the Belgian flag. But by the reign of King Baudouin things had changed.

5

Dipanda

Up to the end of the second World War in 1945, the Congolese in general did not openly resist the Belgian system. There was a strike at the Union Minière in 1941 followed by rioting in Elisabethville (Lubumbashi), a revolt of soldiers at Luluabourg in 1944, and strikes and rioting in Matadi in 1945, but these were only beginnings. The war brought Congo out of its isolation from the rest of the world. African troops had served abroad, bringing white and black shoulder to shoulder in a common cause. No one could escape the worldwide denouncement of the racial doctrines of Nazism. The United Nations had been organized to assure the rights of men everywhere.

Looking at their own country, the Congolese were increasingly aware of things they had been denied. Official Belgian policy said racial discrimination was illegal and punishable, but in actual practice Congolese did not enjoy the same privileges as Europeans. The group to notice this particularly was the *"evolué,"* the elite of Congo who by virtue of their advancement in education and economic status should have been more on a par with Europeans by now. As a reward to Congolese who could prove themselves "civilized" by reason of advanced education, assimilation of European standards of living, and exemplary service, the Belgian Government offered a "civic merit" card, which entitled holders to special privileges. However, those who applied for the card were subjected to such unreasonable examinations and humiliating prying into their personal lives that few obtained it. Those who did found the "civic merit" card still did not give them equal status with Europeans. Wages for blacks—even those who had higher education than their white counterparts—were lower, compulsory labor was required of all Africans, and there were discriminations in the penal code. A much larger percentage of the population now lived in cities— Léopoldville, Elisabethville, Stanleyville, Matadi, and Luluabourg all had a more European than African look—yet primitive village standards of hygiene and housing prevailed for the "natives," elite or not. European and African children went to separate schools; there was little social intermingling, even among the intellectuals. Most of all the Africans resented being treated as children, being called "sons" or "boys," or sometimes "monkeys," and handled as exotic showpieces, as at the Brussels Worlds Fair.

The visit of King Baudouin to Congo in 1955 created quite a stir, for it looked at last as if the Congolese were to be given some responsibility and voice in their own affairs. Some of the Europeans were shocked to see the king shaking hands and mingling freely with the Africans, even pulling up a chair for the wife of one of the men so that she could join in the French conversation more comfortably. "What other white would have done that?" the Congolese asked each other admiringly. The king followed it up in Belgium with a speech calling for better representation of the Congolese in their Government.

Neither African nor Belgian citizens of Congo had political rights, though European administrators of some of the big mining and industrial interests had considerable influence on the Government, as had leaders of the Catholic Church which dominated in Belgium. In response to demands by both black and white, consultative councils were organized, with representatives from both African and European constituencies, but these had no real power in the overall Government.

In 1956, the year after King Baudouin's visit and also, significantly, the year the first Congolese student graduated from a Belgian university, the first important political manifesto of Congo nationalism appeared in a Catholic journal, *Conscience Africaine*. This was partly in response to talk that had been going on for some time about a "Belgo-Congolese Community," an idea put forth by the Belgians of eventually making Congo an equal partner with Belgium rather than a colony. The Congolese were suspicious of how this would work, since none of them had been consulted in the so-called plan. Furthermore, a Belgian professor, Van Bilsen, had published a document in which he put forth a "Thirty-Year Plan for the Political Emancipation of Belgian Africa," urging Belgium to work toward Congo's complete independence. In the political manifesto of 1956 the Congolese said that if the Belgians were really sincere about giving them independence within thirty years, they would cooperate.

All sorts of organizations sprang up: trade unions working for better wages, tribal organizations reviving old history and culture, some political groups. *"Dipanda,"* the Africanized term for "Independence," became the watchword.

One of the first groups to become politically active was ABAKO (Association of the Bakongo), originally organized to preserve the culture of the Bakongo, descendants of the ancient Kingdom of Kongo. Joseph Kasavubu, leader of ABAKO, started pressing for immediate independence rather than a wait of thirty years. His followers took up the cry and dreamed of restoring the old kingdom with Kasavubu on the throne. . . . *"Le Roi . . . Roi Kasa!"* which translates, "The King . . . King Kasa (vubu) !"

A religious organization of Bakongo origin, the Kimbanguists, also had considerable influence in fostering political independence. Since the imprisonment by the Belgians of its founder, Simon Kimbangu, in 1921, the movement had been forced into exile. Even though Kimbangu died in prison, the movement had flourished and some of its adherents—practicing their religion in secret—had important posts in the administration. In 1957 a group of them, led by Kimbangu's son, Joseph Diangenda, openly confronted the Governor General with the hypocrisy of Belgium's declaring itself to believe in the United Nations Charter of the Rights of Man while suppressing Congolese freedom to worship. They demanded that the Governor either tolerate the existence of the Kimbanguist Church—which had been falsely accused of political subversion—or arrest, even kill, them. The Governor could not refuse the former alternative, though he did not officially lift the ban until 1959.

Other political parties appeared, each with their special leaders and objectives: the MNC (Mouvement National Congolaise) was formed in October, 1958, associated with Patrice Lumumba, who was to become the first Prime Minister of the Congo, and also with Albert Kalonji, a powerful figure in the Kasai; CONAKAT (confederation of ethnic associations of Katanga), the party of Moise Tshombe, another future Prime Minister; PNP (Parti National du Progrès), CEREA (Centre de Regroupement Africain) and others. By the time of independence in 1960 there were over forty different political parties, though many of them were small tribal groups. Anyone passing by a meeting of the Lulua Frères (Lulua Brothers) might have seen crowds dancing, playing drums and tshisanji (thumb pianos), singing gaily *"Muoyo Bena Lulua."* But the words to this song were not so gay:

> "Greetings, Lulua people,
> The white people came and put us in a fence,
> We who stand a strong column of the Congo,
> We have our own meetings.
> Our president walks around with white people,
> But our chief Kalamba is only a puppet.
> He is like a leopard
> Who is fed dog meat instead of goat."

It was the ultimate humiliation for a leopard, traditional symbol of royal power, to have to eat dog meat, the food for beggars.

The year 1959 opened with a riot in Léopoldville. Both ABAKO and the Kimbanguists were accused of having started it, though there was no real evidence for this. There was growing unrest all over the Congo over unemployment, poor living conditions, and Belgian domination. The winds of freedom were blowing over Africa: Ghana had become independent in 1957 and was urging other countries to do likewise; three representatives of the MNC, including Patrice Lumumba, had attended the December 1958 conference called by President Nkrumah in Accra and returned announcing that Congo must be independent by 1961. De Gaulle had offered independence to the French Congo across the river.

The Belgians were awakening slowly to the fact that the Congo could not wait "thirty years" for independence and realized, too, that unless they cooperated with the Congolese now, they would be ousted forever. The economy of Belgium depended too much on this colony to let it slip out of their hands thus; besides, there were some Belgian administrators who had been advising earlier independence all along. Plans got underway in 1959 for a general election in Congo in 1960, and, to prepare for it, a Legislative Council was set up in Brussels; this was a sort of Senate to advise on drafting bills for the Congo. A group of 150 Congolese students —some already enrolled in Belgian universities, others brought over especially—became the nucleus of a program in Brussels to train qualified administrators, professional people and technicians for later service in Congo. One of these was Joseph Mobutu, a young journalist who had come to Brussels to work for Congo Information Service.

This training program, however, was too far in the future for the Congo party leaders pushing for immediate action. Finally in late 1959 a Round Table on the Congo was scheduled to be held in Brussels starting on January 20, 1960.

Attending the Round Table Conference, besides the Belgian ministers and members of Parliament, were forty-four Congo delegates representing all the major parties: ABAKO with eleven delegates led by Mr. Kasavubu; CONAKAT with three, led by Mr. Tshombe; P.N.P., eleven; M.N.C., two; eleven representatives from the tribal chiefs, and six delegates from smaller parties. Mr. Lumumba, leader of MNC, was in prison at the time the meeting started, accused of having incited riots in Stanleyville. But there was such a clamor about his absence that he was released and brought over. Already the most powerful orator in Congo, when Patrice Lumumba entered on January 26, displaying the manacle wounds on his wrists, he became the hero and dominating figure at the Round Table Conference. Also he found favor with the Belgians because he was for a united Congo with a strong central government; Tshombe leaned toward a looser organization whereby his rich province, Katanga, could be more independent. Kasavubu, too, was partial to his people, the Bakongo.

The Round Table Conference set June 30, 1960, as the date

for Congo independence and made sixteen resolutions which were later embodied in the Loi Fondamentale (Basic Law) providing the constitution for the new Congo Republic. This Basic Law was passed officially by the Belgian Parliament in May, 1960.

The Congolese were by no means unanimous in how they were going to set up their independence. Tribal fighting—some of the worst of it in the Kasai area, between the Lulua and the Baluba—jealousies between party leaders, jockeying for positions in the new government, all contributed to intense disturbances preceding the general elections to be held in May.

Lumumba's loudspeaker vans traveled all over the Congo and everywhere he went he hypnotized the people; being one of the

Elections, May 1960

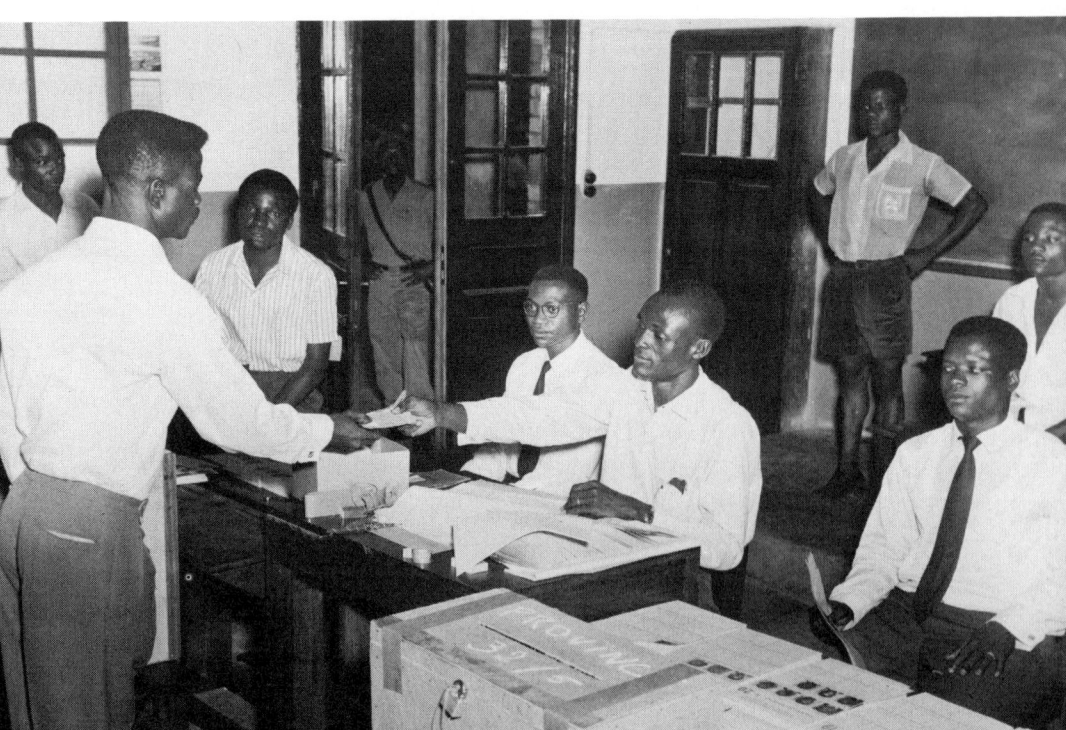

most articulate of the *"evolué"* (the educated elite), detribalized (he came from a small tribe, inactive politically), and also identified with other African nationalists through his contacts at Accra, he had a wide appeal to the masses. In spite of the many party and tribal divisions, Lumumba and the MNC gained an overwhelming victory at the elections.

But though Lumumba's party had won the majority in the May election, the new Government had to represent all parties; Lumumba negotiated with Tshombe, Bolikango, and other party leaders, but failed to secure their cooperation. The Belgian Minister, Walter Ganshof van der Meersch, then asked Kasavubu to try to form a government, which incensed Lumumba. The two Congolese leaders finally patched up their quarrels and agreed to share power: Lumumba as Prime Minister and Kasavubu as President.

Léopoldville was a scene of wild jubilation on June 30, 1960, the birthday of the new Congo republic. Congolese music is reputed to be the most beautiful in Africa and there was no end to special musical compositions for the day. The words to one of them, "Indépendence Cha Cha" covered the Round Table Conference and gave a complete listing of political parties and leaders, all to a "cha cha" bounce and infectious music. In a pageantry of color and special costumes, men, women, and many children danced down Boulevard Albert—later renamed Boulevard du 30 Juin—proclaiming *"Dipanda!"* Congolese dignitaries in top hats and insignia of the royal leopard rolled by in Cadillacs, waving to the screaming throngs. King Baudouin, here for the occasion, also received cheers, though some shouts of *"Vive le Roi!"*[1] were drowned out by *"Vive Kasa, notre Roi."*[2] Most enthusiastic of all were the cries for the

---

[1] "Long live the King!". . . .
[2] "Long live Kasa(vubu), our King."

Congo Independence, June 30, 1960: King Baudouin, President Kasavubu, Prime Minister Lumumba

Prime Minister Lumumba, Colonel Mobutu

Prime Minister, and Lumumba exulted in them. Still smarting at the insult of the Belgian Minister, who had tried to the last to manipulate Congolese, Lumumba turned his speech of welcome to the King of Belgium into an occasion of revenge:

"We are no longer your monkeys!" he shouted to King Baudouin. Later he apologized.

6

From Dipanda to Operation Shirtsleeves

The speech-making and joyful celebration of *Dipanda* soon turned to bloody rioting. Within less than a week the Congolese army, Force Publique, had mutinied and there was panic all over the country. Katanga seceded, tribal fighting rose to a high pitch in the Kasai, and by September, 1960, Prime Minister Lumumba's government collapsed.

The task of moulding together the huge country was formidable, demanding super-human leaders of great wisdom, maturity, and patience. The young republic had only been allowed a few baby steps—these only within the year—before it was thrown out of the Belgian crib on June 30, 1960. An active program to provide higher education and technical training had started too late to have ready the qualified Congolese leaders; there were less than twenty university graduates in the whole country at the time of independence. By contrast, the seven thousand university graduates produced by France in her African colonies must have accounted, at least partially, for their smoother transition to independence. Few of the Congolese were accustomed to thinking in terms of a united nation: many viewed independence simply as a means of taking over the white man's house and jobs and gaining personal or tribal prestige. Even Lumumba at a mellower time had declared that the Congolese only wished to be "Belgians," i.e., to have the same rights and privileges as Belgians. When it became evident that many Congolese wanted these rights and privileges only for themselves or their particular tribal groups, Lumumba shouted: "Down with tribalism and colonialism!"

The whole world was standing by, waiting to see what would happen in the new country. Now that Belgium theoretically was "out," other countries took special interest and offered aid for development. The United States gave a birthday present of three hundred scholarships to American universities and colleges. The rich Katanga area, which already had international interests involved, particularly attracted business concerns, many of which later championed Tshombe's cause in separating it from the republic. Other African countries, particularly Ghana, watched over and at times gave political advice to the new Government.

The day after independence Lumumba applied to the United Nations for membership, declaring Congo ready to accept "without reservation" the obligations of belonging to the world body. A few days later he was raving against Dag Hammarskjold, the UN Secretary General, for remaining neutral in his dispute over Katanga.

Most of the Belgians had remained in Congo and many apparently expected things to go on as usual. The white officials of the Congolese army made this clear, one of the generals writing on a blackboard these words: "Before independence = after independence." Such attitudes triggered the Force Publique mutiny on July 5, spreading riots all over the Congo. The pent-up feelings of many years against white injustice burst into flame, and anti-white sentiment spread in some areas indiscriminately. One of the victims was a young Belgian most beloved by the Congolese, André Ryckmans,

Force Publique (Congolese Army)

son of the former Governor General. His African friends were heartbroken when Ryckmans was found shot by their own bullets during a rescue mission at Thysville. Panic and fear spread through all white settlements, particularly Léopoldville, and there was mass evacuation, airlifts to Europe. Tshombe, often accused of being the pawn of white and business interests, called for Belgian troops to protect the white citizens in Elisabethville. This angered Lumumba, but Tshombe's reply was to declare Katanga independent. UN troops called in by Lumumba were successful in removing most of the Belgian troops, but Katanga remained seceded until the end of the next year, 1961. Meanwhile Lumumba had to quell another rebellion in the South Kasai, led by Albert Kalonji; for this he asked and got some Soviet aid.

In this chaotic state relations between the President and Prime Minister, which had never been good, deteriorated completely. In September, 1960, Kasavubu fired Lumumba, who in turn fired Kasavubu. Then the new young Chief of Staff of the Force Publique, Colonel Joseph Mobutu, fired both of them, announced seizure of the Government and closed parliament. Colonel Mobutu brought in a group of older college students to help with the Government, and the students soon turned to the UN to police the riot-torn country.

Lumumba was under arrest, but his former prime minister deputy, Antoine Gizenga, supported by European Communists took

Refugees in the Kasai, 1960

over Stanleyville in the northwest area of the country and declared it the new capital. Lumumbist anti-Beligan riots also broke out in the eastern province of Kivu.

The mysterious death of Lumumba in or en route to a prison in Katanga in February, 1961, caused worldwide reaction. In spite of his volatile personality and chaotic regime, he had become a symbol of black freedom movements everywhere, a victim of white paternalism, a very gifted man torn between two cultures, belonging to neither. His book, *Congo My Country*,[1] published after his death, reflected Lumumba's genuine and deep concern for his country, as well as his own great insecurity and frustration.

Kasavubu, reinstated as President in January, 1961, appointed Joseph Ileo as Prime Minister, but he was replaced the following April by Cyrille Adoula.

In a continuing attempt to unite Katanga to the republic of Congo, UN Secretary-General Dag Hammarskjold scheduled a meeting with Moise Tshombe in September, 1961. En route to Elisabethville Hammarskjold died in a plane crash. His successor, U Thant, succeeded in ending the Katanga secession by the end of the year, but Tshombe went into exile in Europe.

The regime of Prime Minister Adoula, from 1961 to June 1964, was occupied with continuing army revolts, general strikes, and several rebellions by former Lumumba associates, chiefly Gizenga and Mulele, both with Communist connections. When it finally appeared that the Congo was again headed for anarchy, Adoula was asked to resign and was replaced by Tshombe, brought back from his exile in Europe.

The Tshombe regime of fifteen months succeeded in ending

---

[1] *Le Congo—Terre d'Avenir—Est-il Menacé?* by Patrice Lumumba

temporarily the Lumumbist rebellions, although suppression of a Communist-supported rebellion in Stanleyville, led by Christopher Gbenye, required the use of mercenaries and United States aid. Overlooked in many of the dramatic accounts in international journals of the 1964 rebellion—in which the American doctor, Paul Carlson, was held hostage and later murdered—were the thousands of Congolese who died in equally tragic circumstances.

A power struggle between Kasavubu and Tshombe in October, 1965, ended in Kasavubu once more firing his Prime Minister. Again Joseph Mobutu, now promoted to General of the Congolese army, stepped in. On November 25, 1965, he discharged Kasavubu and proclaimed himself President of an interim government.

President Mobutu abolished all political parties, leaving most of the leaders free and releasing some who had been in prison. A new constitution was adopted in June, 1967, providing for legislative and presidential elections to take place in November, 1970, and also for an opposition party. At present the only recognized party is the MPR, Mouvement Populaire de la Révolution, and a recent statement declared there is no need for any other since the MPR expresses the will of the Congolese people to "live in unity." Most Congolese citizens carry MPR membership cards or wear pins with the party insignia, a hand holding a lighted torch. In the November, 1970 elections President Mobutu was returned to office by an overwhelming vote—not surprising, since he was the only candidate.

Many of the factions and obstacles that plagued the Government of the Democratic Republic of the Congo during its first ten years of independence are gone now: Lumumbist followers have dwindled and split, mercenary troops and some Katangese moved to Rwanda, and Tshombe and Kasavubu both died in 1969. Other opposition leaders, however, such as Munongo and Kalonji Albert, are living quietly in Kinshasa. The fact that plans are underway for constructing a large monument to Lumumba, and that many ideas attributed to him are being incorporated by the present regime indicates that the administration can look objectively and constructively at the past. But much remains to be done to truly unify this huge country with its many kinds of people and many different opinions as to how this should be done. As in all countries of the world, the younger generation, especially those with higher education, are questioning methods and goals of the establishment and demanding their right to be heard. At the same time tribal and old political loyalties, though suppressed, still form an undercurrent of dissent, which cannot be ignored.

At the beginning of his rule in November, 1965, President Mobutu, who has twice pulled the Congo from the brink of disaster, issued an appeal to every Congolese citizen to join hands and work together for the development of the republic: *"Retroussons les manches!"* he challenged: "Let us roll up our sleeves!" And so "Operation Shirtsleeves" goes on, each year announcing a new "revolutionary" goal for achievement.

7

The Government of the Republic

THE NATIONAL ANTHEM

Debout Congolais
Unis par le sort
Unis dans l'effort pour l'indépendance

Dressons nos fronts longtemps courbés
Et pour de bon prenons le plus bel élan
Dans la paix

O peuple ardent,
Dans le labeur
Nous bâtirons un pays plus beau qu'avant
Dans la paix.

   Citoyens .... *citoyens*
   Entonnez .... *entonnez*
   L'hymne sacré de votre solidarité
   Fièrement .... *fièrement*
   Saluez .... *saluez*
   L'emblème d'or de votre souveraineté

Congo
Don béni .... *Congo*
Dex aieux .... *Congo*
O pays .... *Congo*
Bien aimé .... *Congo*

Nous peuplerons ton sol et nous assurerons ta grandeur

Trente juin .... *O doux soleil*
Trente juin .... *du trente juin*
Jour sacré .... *Sois le témoin*
Jour sacré .... *de l'immortel*

Serment de Liberté
Que nous léguons à notre posterité
Pour toujours.

Stand, Congolese
United by destiny
United in the effort for independence

Let us raise our heads long bowed
And for good spring forward with greatest vigor
In peace

O earnest people,
Through work
We will build a country more beautiful than before
In peace

Citizens .... citizens
Sing .... sing
The sacred hymn of your solidarity

Proudly .... proudly
Salute .... salute
The golden emblem of your dominion.

Congo,
Blessed gift .... Congo
Of our ancestors .... Congo
O country .... Congo
Well loved .... Congo

We will people your soil and confirm your greatness

June 30 .... O gracious sun
June 30 .... of June 30
Sacred day .... be the witness
Sacred day .... of the immortal

Pledge of liberty
Which we bequeath to our descendants
Forever.

Anywhere you go in Congo, school children are prepared to give you from memory an ear-splitting rendition of the national anthem, which was written by J. Lutumba, set to music by S. Boka.

The flag of the Republic is blue, representing the sky, with a yellow star in the upper left corner and crossed diagonally by a red band finely edged with yellow. The motto is: Justice, Peace, Work. The coat of arms is composed of a leopard head enclosed on the left with a palm branch and an arrow, and on the right with an ivory tusk and a spear, all resting on a stone.

The Republic today consists of the capital, Kinshasa, and eight administrative provinces: Kongo Central, Équateur, Orientale, Kasai Occidental, Kasai Oriental, Kivu, Bandundu, and Katanga.

Congo flag

Coat of Arms

The New Revolutionary Constitution adopted in April, 1967, provides for a President of the Republic, as Head of Government; Ministers who are heads of various departments: Interior, Foreign Affairs, Territorial Administration, Labor and Housing, Justice, Finance, National Economy and Tourism, Education, Agriculture and Rural Development, Information, Transport and Communication, Mines, Public Health, Public Works, Culture, Youth and Sports; the National Assembly; the Constitutional Court; and the Courts and tribunals.

The Constitution rules against racial, ethnic, or religious discrimination, as well as any organization that might endanger national security. There is no State religion; all three branches of Christianity—Catholic, Protestant, and Kimbanguist—are recognized as are the non-Christian religions. All individual rights are guaranteed. There are also laws governing labor, property ownership, tax, and fiscal regulations.

The political organization, MPR (Mouvement Populaire de la Révolution) with centers all over the Congo, was created by President Mobutu in May, 1967, with the stated objective "to make a really independent country and to restore its international prestige."

Each province has its own capital, governor, and territorial divisions. In the following listing of provincial capitals note a number of names have changed: Bandundu, capital of Bandundu province; Mbuji-Mayi (formerly Bakwanga), Kasai Oriental; Luluabourg, Kasai Occidental; Matadi, Kongo Central; Bukavu, Kivu; Kisangani (Stanleyville), Orientale; Mbandaka, Équateur; and Lubumbashi (Elisabethville), Katanga.

The ANC or National Congolese Army, is still headed officially by Lieutenant-General Joseph Mobutu, but during his current service as President of the Republic, it is under the direct control of the Commander in Chief.

The Banque Nationale du Congo, National Bank of Congo, was constituted and organized by decree on February, 1961, and changed status in June, 1967, when the Zaire (equivalent to U.S. $2) replaced the old Congolese franc. It functions as a central bank for government financial transactions, credit direction, and general transactions as well.

Other deposit banks and financial institutions include: Banque du Congo, Banque Belge d'Afrique, Socobanque (Congolese Bank Association), Credico (Congolese Credit), and Sonas (National Insurance Association).

Legal holidays are: January 1, New Year's; January 4, Martyrs of Independence; Easter Monday; May 1, Labor Day; May 20, anniversary of the founding of the MPR; Ascension Thursday; Monday after Pentecost; June 30, Anniversary of Independence; August 15, Feast of Assumption; November 1, All Saints Day; November 17, National Army Day; November 24, Anniversary of the New Regime; and December 25, Christmas.

Though most of the old party leaders are dead or gone, the present Government is taking no chances on buildup of local power anywhere. Provincial governors and military officials are deliberately assigned outside their home territories: for example, the governor of Orientale Province might be a Swahili-speaking man from Katanga, 500 miles to the south, while the commanding general of the army here might come from Equateur province, far to the west. Theoretically, this is good strategy, but sometimes there are problems. As in colonial times, many tensions and misunderstandings arise when law enforcement officials do not speak the local language or have no respect for local customs. For both the governors and the governed, it is easier to cheat or take advantage of people for whom you feel no personal loyalty.

Some of the officials have been poorly equipped for administrative responsibility, with limited education, little understanding of justice, or an irresponsible attitude to power; some have taken advantage of their positions for personal gain. However, a new type of civil servant is being produced by the Ecole Nationale D'Administration, ENA (formerly ENDA), a school established in 1960 by the Government with aid from the Ford Foundation. ENA graduates and an increasing number of university educated Congolese lawyers are contributing to the constantly improving administration of law and justice.

The policies of the Mobutu regime have been questioned by some who consider them repressive. The national election of November, 1970, was controlled entirely by the MPR, since no other party has been allowed to exist; political opposition has been suppressed. But most people, even Mobutu's enemies, agree that no other man could have restored the Congo to its present healthy state, and some feel that only he can carry it forward to further development.

Law Students

"The most important thing that General Mobutu has done as President of the Congo is to give us a sense of nationhood," said Jean Felix Koli, acting-rector of Université Libre, on the occasion of the Republic's tenth anniversary celebration. "No one ever used to call himself a Congolese. Now we do."

The one-party, one-man government system is not unique to Congo. Some of the most enlightened African governments—Tanzania and Zambia, for example—have been using one-party rule successfully for some time. How well it works for Congo will depend on how wisely the administration responds to its people's desires to have a voice in their own development. Good-natured and tolerant as most Congolese are, they are also very open in expressing opinions about things, pro and con. So it is quite unnatural for them to have to refrain from critical remarks for fear of being accused of "subversion," or lack of patriotism, or for fear of losing jobs. Members of certain clans or tribal groups sometimes complain of discrimination. Ambitious younger, university-educated Congolese have expressed discouragement about their role in the Congo's future, since it appears to them that little is being done to encourage new political leaders.

There are signs that the administration is aware of these voices of discontent and that it recognizes the need not only for a firm and guiding hand, but also breathing and growing room for all of Congo's many kinds of people, who want a share in their own development.

8

The People

The people of the Congo are as varied as the land. From the four-foot-tall Pygmies to the seven-foot Watusi, they are of all sizes, shapes, and colors: some have round faces, wide-set eyes, generous mouths and are stockily built, while others are tall and slender, with high foreheads and fine features; some have dark black skin, others are reddish brown; some move quickly, with great energy, while others take their time. Perhaps their most universal characteristics are gaiety, a marvelous ability to laugh at themselves as well as at others, and a tremendous loyalty to those they respect as "brothers," either through blood ties or through personal choice.

"Speak to the wise man in proverbs," they say. "To the idiot one must speak openly." Many foreign "idiots" miss a great deal because they cannot understand the proverbs (which lose much in translation). In every dialect, for instance, there are picturesque warnings against false pride or over-ambition:

> "He who talks about a stranger, today it is of him they are talking."

> "Little wren, take on what is your size,
> Don't try to imitate the eagles or the owls."

Students at Associated School of the Institut Chrétien Congolais, Bolenge

The Pygmies, earliest known inhabitants of Congo—arrived in this area perhaps 20,000 years ago—live largely in the northern forest regions of the Ituri, in the inter-lake region of the Kivu, on the borders of Lake Léopold II, the Sankuru River and in the Ubangi plains. Because of their tendency to isolate themselves in the forest, they are still the least influenced by modernization. But Bantu invasions and intermarriages are changing them, too.

The Sudanese predominate in the northern region bordering Sudan; the main tribal groups are Zande and Mangbetu.

Hamitic and Nilotic people are generally in the eastern part of the country: the tall Watusi, who are Hamitic refugees from neighboring Rwanda, live in the Kivu, while such Nilotic people

Pygmy Village in the Ituri Forest

as the Alur, Bari, Lugwara, and Logo occupy lands of the northeast corner of Congo, and the length of Lake Albert. These people speak a form of Swahili, and compose about 3 percent of the total population.

The bulk of the population, about 70 percent, belongs to the Bantu group. Some of the main tribal divisions are settled as follows:

Central Congo: The Bakongo
Along the Congo River: the Bateke, Mongo, Turumbu, Ngombe, Babali, Mongelima
Ubangi: (northwest corner): the Bangala
Northeast: the Babua

Lake Region: the Baniari, Bashi (central Kivu), Kabare, Babira (Ituri), Bakumu, Wanianga, Bahunde

Along the Lomami and Lulualaba rivers: the Topoke, Lokele, Mituku, Wasongola, Bango-Bango

South and Center: (Katanga and Kasai provinces: Baluba, Bakualulua, Basongo, Batetela, Balunda, Bakuba)

Lake Mwero: Bayeke, Baushi, Balomotwa, Tshokwe

Kwilu and Kwango: Basuku, Bayaka, Bapende

In spite of these many tribal divisions, cultural patterns are surprisingly uniform for this huge country. All the people practice agriculture, though there is more emphasis on hunting and fishing in the forest regions—among the Pygmies and the Mongo, for example—than in the northern and southern plain regions, separated by the forests. Cattle-raising is practiced mainly in the eastern highlands, though there is a large cattle ranch in the vicinity of Matadi (near the west coast).

"When God made Adam and Eve, He gave Eve a hoe and told her to go to the field and dig. He gave Adam a pipe and told him to sit at home and smoke."

Many Congolese males support this unorthodox Christianized version of the traditional role of women, but they get by with it in actual practice only in the hinterlands where the women don't know that things have changed. Walking along the winding roads of the Kivu mountains or in a remote forest area of Équateur province, one can see women with huge loads of wood strapped to their backs or tremendous loads of manioc sticks balanced on their heads, while men saunter by, both hands free. Some claim the man walks ahead ready to protect women from danger; therefore he must be unencumbered, ready to go into action.

*Lalia hunter
of Equator Province*

Children in traditional Congo society learn their roles early. Living in a small village where everyone is "kin" of some sort, they receive their training from a number of people beside their immediate parents.

Though most families are large—twelve or thirteen is not unusual—every child that arrives gets his due share of attention, with a naming ceremony, elaborate rites, feasting and dancing. A traditional birth song among the Baluba, "Tuai Kankanene," hails the child, points out his mother and all the members of the community who will be responsible for his upbringing and then threatens him that if he cries too much he will have to cook the manioc greens. Congolese children are not coddled; most of them walk well before they are a year old, and since the mothers generally have to give their attention soon to younger children or to domestic duties, the toddlers are put out into the group quite early to fend for themselves. However, there is always an older brother or sister around to pick up or help them if the mother is otherwise occupied.

From the age of five or six until twelve, girls receive special training from their mothers and female members of the village in domestic science, food raising, and duties relating to marriage and motherhood. The boys are trained by the men of the community in the masculine arts of hunting, fishing, field clearing, and special crafts. At the age of puberty, there are separate initiation

Boy fishing on the Congo River

rites for girls and boys, at which time they are proclaimed adults. The girl is then ready for marriage, her father sets a bridal price, and the husband applicants start coming. Often the girl and the boy agreed upon for her mate have little choice in the matter, depending on what ambitions their parents may have. The dowry paid by the groom generally consists of a certain number of goats, chickens, copper crosses—in the old days, "nzimbu"—or perhaps an even exchange of another marriageable girl. Some brides are considered worth more if they have had some Western education, but on the other hand some men prefer women without this kind of education, because they are easier to control.

Birth, initiation, and marriage customs vary a great deal from one tribe to another, often depending on the local custom of family lineage.

Most of the societies adopt a system of lineage from one parent: e.g., in a patrilinear society, a person is a member of a group formed by all the descendants of males only from a common ancestor. In this case brothers and sisters belong to the same group, but the children of sisters don't count. In a matrilinear society, found largely in the southern plains, a person counts his lineage only from the women in the family. This makes for a lot of complication in figuring out who your relatives are and which of them you can afford to ignore.

As the Congo becomes more modernized, some of these traditions are becoming less important, especially with the deliberate suppression of tribalism in the interest of national unity.

However, these old customs and loyalties still persist, not always under the surface. A young woman cannot ignore the uncle on her mother's side who doesn't like the young man she has chosen for a husband; the uncle's dislike could be intensified if the groom fails to pay the dowry or ignores other traditions. When

Congo fashion models

such a young woman defies her uncle to marry the man of her choice, she must be prepared to face the "curses," real or imagined, he may threaten to bring down upon her; she can be blamed for sickness or death in the family brought on—her uncle says—by angry ancestors. Congolese are blessed, or cursed, with an infinite number of people who are related to them by blood or by membership in the same clan. Traditionally it is unheard of to turn away such a "relative" if he comes to you for help. Congolese living in tiny, crowded apartments in Washington, Brussels, or in Kinshasa, must often welcome relatives who arrive uninvited for an indefinite stay. A young man who chooses a foreign bride—for example, an American, a Belgian, or a Haitian—must make sure she has the stamina and devotion to listen to endless hours of advice on what is expected of a Congo wife (if her husband is the eldest son, for example, she must assume responsibility for all his younger brothers and sisters, as well as for any children she may bear herself).

A school child told this story illustrating the importance of family ties in the Congo:

One day the chicken went to the river to draw water. Suddenly as she was leaning over the edge of the water, a crocodile came up.

"Oh, what a wonderful feast we will have today!" cried the crocodile. "My wife is going to have babies and has eaten no meat for months, but tonight she will eat chicken!"

But the chicken exclaimed: "You, child of the family of my parents and of my grandparents, are you treating me like a special prize for your wife? Are we not descended from the same ancestor?"

Surprised, the crocodile answered: "But I live in the waters and my body is covered with scales. My teeth chew only flesh. How can I be of the same race as you?"

Then the crocodile grabbed the chicken and carried her home. When he got home, the crocodile discovered that his wife had laid three eggs.

That evening the chicken laid some eggs and put them under the crocodile, while she brought the crocodile eggs to her own nest. So the next morning the crocodile had hatched chickens and the chicken had hatched crocodiles. Everyone was quite amazed.

At last the crocodile believed that he was from the chicken family, in spite of the fact that they had feathers and a beak, and that they lacked the teeth to chew flesh.

So the crocodile let go his cousin chicken.

9

Religion

NZAMBI OF THE AFRICANS

"It is Nzambi who prepares the manioc bread; we men prepare only the seasonings."

So goes an old Bakongo proverb. "Nzambi," "Nzambe," "Maweja," "Nvidi Mukulu" are various names given to a Supreme Being believed in by all people of the Congo from ancient times to the present. In the ancient religions—which continue to be practiced as animism in some degree by perhaps half the people, God is a powerful source of all being, generally far off and accessible through lesser spirits dwelling in nature or in ancestors. Forests, animals, birds, trees, all contain these spirits and therefore must be respected and obeyed. In some sections, for example, the python and rainbow represent symbols of fertility: a part of the field is left uncultivated as a shelter for the mythical snake who will bring good harvests. Everywhere the leopard is associated with power and in some areas no one but a chief would dare sit on a leopard skin.

Masks, effigies, shrines, all sorts of sacred objects are made to house the spirits of nature or the departed souls of ancestors. Diviners and medicine men (and women) often play an important role in helping people deal with the spirits, establishing communica-

Baluba tribesman in ceremonial dress

tion with the supernatural world, making charms and prescribing medicines to ward off sickness and death. These medicine men often have real knowledge of practical remedies for sickness, such as healing herbs, which they combine with psychological skill to effect cures. Every event of life, whether it is birth, an initiation ceremony at adolescence, celebration of a successful hunt, or a death, has a religious implication, for the Congolese truly believe there is a vital force in everything. Through the complicated, often very elaborate ritual ceremonies, generally involving sacrifice, music, and dancing, there are simple prayers to the Supreme Being. Here is a Lulua prayer asking "Nvidi Mukulu" for food:

> "Goodness! God of Tshiame
> Our fathers had at least the small game.
> You gave us strong teeth to eat with,
> Then why don't you give us to eat?"

Here is one of praise:

> "Lord God of Love, Great God,
> Man looks at the sun and burns his eyes
> So also thy greatness blinds us thus.
> As the little red ant
> Walks in the light rain in the path.
> Great God,
> He cannot look at thy face.
> If he should see thee
> Tears would fall from his eyes."

NZAMBI OF FOREIGNERS—CHRISTIANITY

Besides those who still believe basically in animism today, or who profess no religion, between 30 percent and 40 percent of the population is Christian; about 115,000 belong to Islam, residing mostly in the Maniema district below Kisangani; there are some 2,000 Jews, with a synagogue in Lubumbashi; and a few Pakistani and Indian inhabitants belong to the Ismaelite religion. By far the most influential religious group is the Christian, since their mission schools have provided the early education of most of the present leaders of the country.

Christianity is represented in the Democratic Republic of Congo today by three major groups: Catholics, Protestants, and Kimbanguists. As mentioned in an earlier chapter, the inhabitants of the Kingdom of Kongo accepted readily the Christian religion brought by the Portuguese explorers of 1482. For them Christianity was identified with many benefits to be had from Europe, not the least of which was a means of modernizing their country. Some thought simply of adding Christian practices to their ancestral traditions, for was it not the same Nzambi they had always known? But the missionaries allowed none of the old ways: idols and fetishes had to be burned, "heathen" practices abandoned. The first Mani-Kongo to become Christian, baptized as Joao I, got so much criticism from his subjects because he had abandoned the old customs that he renounced his "conversion" and returned to the religion of his people.

However, his successor, Alfonso I, not only embraced Christianity for himself, attributing a successful military feat to the miraculous intervention of the apostle James, but worked his entire reign to extend the practice of Christianity to his subjects. He was disillusioned finally when the Christian missionaries themselves, priests and bishops, engaged in the most un-Christian practice of slavery and actually contributed to the degradation of his people.

While the Bakongo became disillusioned with the European apostles of Christianity, they retained some of the essential doctrines and began making African adaptations; sometimes they used Christianity as a weapon against its false white prophets.

In 1704 a young Mukongo woman named Kimpa Vita, started a movement that was for several years a rallying force for the tottering Kingdom of Kongo. Kimpa Vita, later known as Dona Beatriz—shown in a European portrait of that time as a slender, fine-featured woman wearing a green robe and a gold crown—

had a vision in which St. Anthony appeared to her on her deathbed. According to her story, she died and St. Anthony entered her head in place of her soul, and thereafter acted through her body. The "saint" set about rallying the Bakongo to rebuild the earthly kingdom, predicting that Judgment was near. Everywhere Dona Beatriz went, nobles venerated her and legends spread about her power over nature: twisted, fallen trees straightened as she passed, they said. She reenacted many of the parts of the Christian story, "dying" every Friday, being "born again" each Saturday, going up to heaven to plead the cause of the Negroes against the whites. When she, though unmarried, gave birth to a son, she proclaimed that it came from God. This story was used against her as more and more of her proclamations proved false. When she was brought up for trial the question was asked: "How could St. Anthony bear a child?" She was exposed as a deceiver of the people and condemned to death.

In a scene very reminiscent of the young Joan of Arc, heroine of fifteenth-century France, Dona Beatriz was burned at the stake in 1706. She died with her child in her arms and the name of Jesus on her lips. Her followers, Antonians or "little Anthonys," continued the movement for several years, proclaiming Kongo as the true Holy Land. They claimed that Christ was born in São Salvador rather than Bethlehem, and taught that white people were made of an inferior kind of soft stone, while blacks originated from a special kind of fig tree. To set themselves apart, Antonians dressed in a special cloth made of fig bark. The rich objects of the whites, they said, would come to all who truly believed in their movement.

Over two hundred years later, Simon Kimbangu, also a Mukongo, was to establish a much stronger, more lasting movement founded on Christianity and also a reaction against white corruption of its essential message.

When the famous Protestant missionary, David Livingstone, discovered the Congo, there began a trek of Protestant representatives from Britain and America and some of the Protestant nations of Europe. One of the best known of these early missionaries was the Baptist pioneer, George Grenfell. Increasing numbers of Catholic missionaries came, largely from France and Belgium. A photo of the first Belgian missionary, Aimé Vyncke, who established a church at Boma in 1884, shows him seated in a chair; a Congolese, dressed in elaborate pantaloons and vest, his hand placed stiffly upon the priest's shoulder, stands respectfully behind him.

The Christian missionaries came supposedly to bring a message of revealed Truth, which emphasized direct access to God, love, and the brotherhood of man. Though they taught that all men are equal in the sight of God, their message often became distorted because they were ignorant of, or lacked respect for, the existing values in Congo civilization. Too, Belgium's King Leopold II recognized that the missionaries could be a valuable force in subjugating the Congolese to suit his own plans. Though himself a Protestant, Leopold II gave special privileges to the Catholic leaders —mostly Belgian—who did not speak out against his abuses. Some of the Protestant leaders—among them William Morrison and William Sheppard of the American Presbyterian Mission—were instrumental in bringing about the international investigation in 1904 which finally brought about the end of the abuses, as well as of Leopold's private ownership of Congo.

The Catholic Church was one of three dominant forces of the Belgian colonial regime, the other two being the State and Big Business. Six of the country's thirteen legal holidays today are connected with events on the Christian calendar. The Catholics built the first university in Congo (Lovanium) and initiated many other programs beneficial to Congo.

Most Congolese acknowledge their debt to the missionaries—Catholic and Protestant—for the schools, hospitals, social programs, and many things that would have been impossible without their help. From the beginning the foreign representatives of Christianity have been of several types: some concerned principally with "saving souls" and supplanting paganism, and others concerned also with man's needs of body, mind, and spirit. The typical pioneer missionary of the latter type not only preached the Christian gospel; he organized schools, wrote books, set broken bones, delivered babies, built houses, and taught farming. No matter how limited his train-

Catholic mission school

ing or equipment, he did whatever had to be done, for there was no one else to do it. Later on, there was specialization: missionary doctors, teachers, architects, industrial or agricultural experts arrived and set the pattern for many of the institutions on which the Congo depends today.

One of the most notable examples of missionary-Congolese collaboration is the newest of Congo's three universities, the Free University of Kisangani, founded by Protestants. After two evacuations because of rebel wars, a second-generation American missionary, Benjamin Hobgood, in 1967, led back a group of Congolese who insisted on another try. Today the university is thriving with over five hundred students, an international faculty of all faiths, including atheists, and plans are underway for major architectural expansion; these plans are being developed by an American architect, the son of former missionaries, and are being funded by an American foundation.

The Catholic university of Lovanium was a pioneer in higher education of Congolese, which precipitated the movement for independence.

On the other hand, the church has been guilty too often of imposing a total way of life, allowing little room for individual interpretation of Christian practice. In initial contacts with Congolese, the Christian missionaries created a great deal of confusion because of their ignorance and insensitivity to the culture of the people. Dr. David McLean, a former missionary now teaching anthropology in the United States, told a story of the misunderstanding he himself caused in his first efforts to speak a local language, Tshiluba, without knowledge of the correct tones. The Tshiluba word for "nose" is the same as that for "heaven"; both are spelled *diulu,* but the vocal tones used in pronunciation are quite different.

Unaware of this, Dr. McLean kept praying publicly, "Our Father Who art in the Nose," giving the impression to Congolese that the new God he was teaching them about lived in human nostrils.

"Pagan" fetishes—carved images of ancestors which were often beautiful works of art—were destroyed because of their association with animism; they were replaced with cheap tin medals of Christian saints and membership cards, which had similar superstitious significance for the Africans. All music and dancing associated with "heathen" rituals was frowned upon. Christian services were a dull replica of those in European or American churches, with slow, staid hymns sung to a wheezy, foot-pumped organ; a washed, dutiful congregation listening patiently to sermons from the pulpit in their own language or to chanting in Latin.

Not all Christian missionaries were this insensitive. Far back in the fifteenth and sixteenth centuries Bakongo Christians were inspired and encouraged to adapt their traditional artistic skills to express their faith, resulting in some very fine frescoes and statuettes of thoroughly African style. *Bantu Philosophy*, a book written in 1945 by Placide Tempels—a Franciscan monk living in Congo many years—gave foreigners new insight into Africa and inspired more missionary acceptance of African traditions. A Kasai Christmas service became a joyful, meaningful occasion when the guiding missionary "allowed"—actually encouraged—dancing and singing a traditional birth song, adapting words about the birth of the Christ Child. The internationally appreciated *Missa Luba* and *Missa Kwango* and other Congolese masses are examples of blending traditional elements into Christianity.

In spite of these efforts to make Christianity relevant to the needs and traditions of the African people, and in spite of the benefits of literacy, health, and general welfare brought by most of the mission programs, for too many Congolese it was a system imposed by white people, often to the exclusion of black values.

THE KIMBANGUISTS

In 1921, Simon Kimbangu, a Baptist-educated young Mukongo, born in the village of Nkamba near Thysville, responded to a vision in which he had been commanded to serve as a special witness for Christ. Leaving his work in the field, he began preaching and healing in the name of Jesus Christ, effecting miraculous cures. He was first suspected of sorcery but, Bible in hand, Kimbangu insisted that it was only Christ's power working through him. Soon many people were leaving their forced labor, their fields and their white masters to go hear the prophet at Nkamba; twelve people, including some women, became his special disciples who also had gifts of healing. Though Kimbangu consistently maintained that he was a mere servant of Christ, neither Catholics nor Protestants would acknowledge him, for they could not control him—this was a totally African movement. Soon the Belgian administration, warned by Catholic missionaries that a revolt of Bakongo was being brewed by the prophet, arrested and imprisoned Simon Kimbangu, only six months after the beginning of his mission. Nkamba was destroyed and Kimbangu's followers were forced to build houses there for soldier guards; however, the prophet's followers refused money for this work, saying they did not want to "sell Nkamba to the Belgians."

A death sentence imposed on Kimbangu was commuted by King Albert to life imprisonment, and he proved such a model prisoner that the province governor and the prison authorities in Katanga, where he was held, sought to release him in 1935. But a Catholic archbishop advised against it, declaring it would mean a spread of the Kimbanguist "heresy" over the Congo. The prophet died in prison on October 12, 1951.

Before he died, Simon Kimbangu designated his youngest son, Joseph Diangenda, as his successor. At the time of their father's imprisonment, Joseph and his brother Charles, then small boys, had been placed in a Catholic institution, where they received their education.

With the suppression of the movement, thousands of families went into exile but, praying and singing their hymns in the forest, the followers of Kimbangu grew in numbers and in spiritual strength. By the time the ban was lifted in 1959, through a confrontation of the Belgian administration by Joseph Diangenda and a group of influential Kimbanguists, *"L'Église de Jésus Christ sur terre par le prophète Simon Kimbangu"* (The Church of Jesus Christ on earth by the prophet Simon Kimbangu) was a strongly developed organization.

Though nonpolitical, according to the precepts of the founder, the Kimbanguist church became a vital force in the movement for independence. In 1959, two photos were circulated among the Bakongo, one showing Christ giving a key of political power to an African man, the other showing Christ laying his hands on the same man. The African man was said to be Kasavubu, leader of the Abako party, who was receiving power from Christ at the request of Simon Kimbangu; some said the prophet had come back to life.

Such stories and exaggerated accounts of the strange rituals developed by the Kimbanguists during their period of exile opened the way for new condemnation of the Kimbanguists both by the Government and the established Christian churches, but not enough now to suppress a movement that had Christianized African traditions and made an independent African church, founded and directed by Africans. Christianity as interpreted by the Kimbanguists was more relevant to many Congolese than it had ever been before.

Joseph Diangenda, the spiritual head of the church—known as "Son Éminence"—lives simply in a modest house in the heart of Kinshasa, receiving thousands of Congolese who crowd daily into the courtyard for individual counselling, prayer, and healing of body and mind; he also spends part of his time at Nkamba/Jerusalem, which has become a place of pilgrimage, as well as a training center. A mausoleum containing the earthly remains of the prophet is situated at the top of a hill just above the long steps down which Kimbangu was led to prison after his arrest.

Joseph Diangenda conducting a Kimbanguist service

Anyone entering a Kimbanguist church—whether the large cathedral in Kinshasa or the holy compound at Nkamba—is immediately overwhelmed with the pageantry and the beauty of the music. Well ordered groups of laymen, women, youths, and children, dressed in military-style uniforms of green and white, stand at attention, as each person removes his shoes and enters the church. Masses of choirs, bands of drummers and flute players erupt into music all through the service, and the congregation itself joins in, without cue or written guide, singing most movingly the prayers and songs of exile. A part of each service is the welcome to strangers, who today might be of almost any nationality, for since its admission to the World Council of Churches in August, 1969, the Kimbanguist Church has attracted worldwide attention. Unlike many other African-organized churches, it is nontribal and its membership, now numbering in the millions, extends to countries outside the Democratic Republic of the Congo.

Though divided in the past, the three branches of Christianity in the Congo—Catholic, Protestant, and Kimbanguist—are working in closer cooperation today than ever before. This is possible because the older mission groups are accepting more completely the idea of a truly African Christian church, not a white-dominated one.

A recent editorial in the journal, *Congo-Afrique,* estimated that 91 percent of the population of Kinshasa are nominally Christian and that approximately 90 percent of the reading public of the country also profess some adherence to Christianity. The accuracy of such figures would have to be determined by what is meant by "Christian"; a person calling himself Christian, for social or business reasons, might still engage in polygamy or ancestor worship; a government official often seen participating in a Christian service, and known to have genuine Christian convictions, might also be observed at a state dinner pouring out a libation—on the side—

for a departed ancestor. Whatever the realities, there is no question of the influence of Christianity on the general thinking of the country, and on the educational and social structure. The *Congo-Afrique* editorial, remarking on the beginning of the fifth year of the *nouveau regime* of President Mobutu in November, 1969, went on to suggest that the moral and spiritual force of Christianity could be a vital factor in helping the republic achieve its goal of national unity.

10

Education and Health

"Educate your children!" shout the red-lettered banners floating over Kinshasa streets; at every educational institution in the country long lines wait patiently to register or inquire about scholarships. Equally long lines wind around the hospitals and clinics of the cities and villages, the improvised dispensaries in the bush, doling out medicine and advice on child care.

For everyone knows that without educated, technically trained and healthy *citoyens* (citizens), the Congo will continue to depend heavily on outsiders for the expertise and energy needed to develop her vast resources.

Educated Congolese have been back of most of the major developments toward a stronger, self-sufficient country: graduation of the first students from Lovanium University in 1958 speeded equalization of wages for Africans and Europeans; the educated *evolué* pioneered moves for independence; young men and women returning from studies abroad are introducing new ideas as they fill important posts in government, teaching, or industry. A recent issue of the journal *Zaire* devotes the cover and a long article to Congolese surgeons.

By the time of independence in 1960, the primary education program of Congo was one of the best in Africa, reaching more than 70 percent of the children between six and eleven years of age, but secondary schools, on the other hand, reached less than 2 percent of their age group, while higher education was barely beginning —Lovanium University at Léopoldville (Kinshasa) and the Official University at Elisabethville (Lubumbashi) were only a few years old. The Belgians had discouraged students going abroad. Thus, while Congo was credited with one of the highest literacy rates in Africa, it really meant only that more people there had had a few years of school. In actual fact, few people had a working knowledge of reading and writing, and a mere handful had university education.

With the end of the Belgian regime there was a tremendous drive for higher education. Offers of scholarships came in from all over the world, and for several years these attracted most of the young Congolese qualified for advanced study; the turbulence and unrest following independence made it preferable to study outside the country.

But, despite the turmoil of the first years, the old education system in the country did not break down completely, and now with increasing stability, tremendous advances have been made. The United Nations, with the help of some individual countries—notably Belgium and the United States—has had a major part in this advance. More Congolese are going to school today—in and out of the country—than ever before. Over half the 19 million inhabitants are under twenty years of age.

All schools operate today under the Ministry of National Education and consist basically of two types: official and independent. Independent institutions include those run and partly financed by the Catholic and Protestant missions, and by the Kimbanguists; these also receive government subsidy. All primary schools are free.

After completing six years of primary school, Congolese children

National Library of Congo (Bibliotheque Nationale du Congo)

are given orientation of two years toward a field in which they want to specialize, such as teaching, mechanics, or general studies leading to law or medicine. Then, after studying in one of these fields for perhaps four years, they have a choice of many postsecondary schools.

UNIVERSITIES

The Congo has three universities, located in different parts of the country: University of Lovanium at Kinshasa, the Official University in Lubumbashi, and the Free University at Kisangani.

Though all three of these offer—or plan to offer—a complete curriculum and are open to all faiths, there are certain traditions and emphases associated with each.

The oldest and best established is the University of Lovanium, founded in 1954 by the Catholics and modeled after the University of Louvain in Belgium. It has a high percentage of Belgian faculty, though the rector is Congolese, and retains a rather formal European structure; this university is particularly strong in medicine and science, administering one of the largest general hospitals in the Congo, and possessing one of the first atomic reactors in the world.

The Université Officielle du Congo (Official University of Congo), located in the mining center of Katanga, emphasizes mining and industry. It, too, has a Congolese rector with a large percentage of foreign professors. It was founded in 1956 at Elisabethville, later to be known as Lubumbashi.

The Université Libre or Free University, has special objectives of local and international service. Founded by Protestants in 1963,

Professor of Universite Libre (Free University), Kisangani

this university was driven twice from its campus by the rebellion in the Stanleyville (now Kisangani) area, taking shelter temporarily at Lovanium University. Since its permanent return to Kisangani in 1967, the Free University has, through the steady determination of a few dedicated leaders—most of them Congolese—and increasingly enthusiastic support from the Government, become a vital force for restoration of this war-torn area in the Congo. It is attracting international interest today as a truly African university, with a faculty over 50 percent African, and with a curriculum being developed to meet Congo's needs and aspirations.

Exchange programs with foreign schools are underway in all three of Congo's universities.

OTHER SPECIAL SCHOOLS AND INSTITUTIONS

Besides the universities, other specialized schools—many of them run by church groups or on foundations of former mission institutions—provide postsecondary education such as pre-university courses, teacher training, theology, or medicine. The *Congo Polytechnic Institute* (Institut Polytechnique du Congo), organized by the Congo Protestant Council, is an example of a school combining university preparation with accelerated courses in agriculture, domestic science, mechanics, public health, social work, etc.

Out of the large variety of specialized schools, comments on only a few can be made here: The *National School of Administration* (Ecole Nationale d'Administration), known as ENA, developed largely by Ford Foundation money and staff soon after independence, trains administrators and magistrates for government service. Graduates are required to remain in government service for a minimum of six years and thus are largely responsible for the constantly improving quality of civil service. *The National Pedagogical Institute* (Institut Pedagogique National) is funded by the Congo Government and the United Nations, with some further financing from Britain, Germany, Belgium, and the U.S.A., and technical help from UNESCO. This institute trains teachers for national schools, working through a pilot secondary training school. It also helps individual institutions improve the quality of their personnel. The *National Institute of Building and Public Works* and *The National Institute of Mining* (Institut National des Mines) train technicians and foremen in specialized fields. *The Higher Institute of Architecture* is a part of the *Academy of Fine Arts* (Academie des Beaux Arts) in Kinshasa, which also offers courses in art and sculpture.

Several institutions function directly under the very active Ministry of Culture and Fine Arts: *The National Conservatory of Music and Drama* (Conservatoire National de Musique et Drame) is one of the most recently established.

MEDICINE AND HEALTH PROGRAM

The National Institute of Medical Training (Institut D'Enseignement Medical) provides training for hospital administration and medical assistants and gives some diplomas in medicine. The World Health Organization, UNESCO, and the International Red Cross provide medicine and teachers and the United States has given money for some buildings.

The Congo Government and the Government of Denmark cooperate in a national medical teaching hospital, the *Clinique Danoise,* in Kinshasa, which trains nurses, anesthetists, and other medical technicians. Many of the mission hospitals throughout the country also have teaching programs.

Thus an ever-growing number of Congolese doctors and nurses —trained at home and abroad—are staffing the many hospitals, dispensaries, and health programs scattered through the country.

Clinique Reine Elisabeth (Queen Elisabeth Clinic) Kinshasa

Equally important, the training of administrators, technicians, and practical nurses has made it possible to improve the quality and variety of health care, such as: rehabilitation centers, maternity hospitals, child care centers, tuberculosis sanatoriums, leprosy camps, and fights against age-old plagues of the Congo, such as malaria and sleeping sickness.

The World Health Organization (WHO) plays a particularly important role in Congo's health program, providing doctors, technicians, and administrators for institutions and programs in the country, as well as scholarship aid for medical students. WHO operates a pilot health center at N'Djili near Kinshasa, this serving as a model for centers throughout the country. Congo also receives technical medical assistance from Belgium, France, from the Swiss Red Cross, Danish Red Cross, and from Foreami. Many industrial concerns operate their own clinics and pharmacies.

In spite of all these efforts and significant progress, health problems are far from solved. Hospitals and clinics all over the country are overcrowded, and many remote areas are without any medical care. The need for more staff, equipment, and funds is great. A very few doctors—Congolese and foreign—enjoy private practices and their own clinics which can provide relative ease and security, but most doctors—black and white—devote the major part of their waking (and sleeping) time to the care of Congo's sick. *Zaire*'s article on surgeons tells of a Congolese doctor performing five Caesarean operations a day as well as administering a hospital accommodating one thousand patients, in space originally designed for four hundred.

11

Diamonds in the Dirt

The moon shines brightly on the Congo River, dimming the man-made radiance of Kinshasa on one side and Brazzaville on the other. A long, slender canoe, poled by a bare-chested fisherman, glides silently into a dark palm-clustered cove far up from the Otraco docks on the Kinshasa side. The fisherman steps lightly to the shore, rustles briefly in the trees, then hops back into the canoe and pushes out into the river. Immediately a shot rings out from a lurking motorboat, which with a mighty roar overtakes the canoe. A few minutes later the picturesque fisherman is hauled, manacled, up the bank, to a waiting police car; triumphant officers follow carrying a bag of diamonds that would have reached Brazzaville within a half hour, had they not intercepted.

Diamond smuggling has stripped Congo of millions of zaires worth of potential wealth. Near the mines at Mbuji Mayi in the Kasai, it is possible to pick up diamonds lying loose in the dirt. Squatters hide in river caves and make away with bags full of the gems, which they pass on through a highly developed system of international illegal trade. This traffic has necessitated very strict regulations and searches at all travel terminals, as well as an enforced law requiring work permits of all Congo residents.

In spite of the loss through smuggling, the Democratic Republic

Diamond Mines at Mbuji-Mayi

of Congo is the world's largest single producer of industrial diamonds, accounting in 1965 for over half the estimated world production.

Copper is an even more important export, accounting in 1968 for almost 62 percent of the Congo's total exports. Other important minerals are cobalt, uranium, tin, and zinc. There is some gold and silver, but in declining quantities.

Since the establishment of the Union Minière du Haut Katanga in the regime of Leopold II, there have been a number of changes in the administration and control of the mineral industry. Union

Minière was nationalized by the Congo Government on December 31, 1966, and a new company, GECOMIN (Société Generale des Congolais des Minerais) replaced it; GECOMIN is completely owned and controlled by the Congo Government. In February, 1967, a five-year agreement was signed between GECOMIN and a Belgian-based company, SGM (Société Generale des Minerais) to cooperate in the operation of the Katanga mines and in the international marketing of copper.

The diamond mine industry, centered in the Kasai, is controlled by MIBA (Société Minière de Bakwanga), in which the Congo Government has 50 percent participation; financial and management control are under a Belgian company, SIEBEKA (Société d'Enterprise et d'Invessements du Beceka).

The two leading tin producers are SYMETAIN (Syndicat Minière d'Étain) and GEOMINES (Compagnie Géologique et Minière), both Belgian controlled.

The soil of Congo produces agricultural riches increasingly important, both for domestic consumption and for export. Making a remarkable comeback from the troubled years, since 1965 the agricultural production has increased over 80 percent. Main exports are palm products, coffee, and rubber, but cotton is coming back as an important crop.

Large foreign-owned plantations produce approximately 80 percent of the palm products; one of the largest and oldest firms is Lever Brothers, manufacturers of Palmolive soap. Foreign-owned coffee plantations, found largely in the Kivu area, have not fully recovered from war ravages, and export has been handicapped by transport problems. Illegal coffee smuggling through the east borders of the Congo has reduced the supply, but, in spite of this, coffee shipments increased 18 percent during 1968. Rubber,

Cotton growers in Uele district of Orientale (Eastern) Province

tea, cocoa, and sugar are also largely produced by foreign-owned companies.

Cotton is produced and processed almost exclusively by Africans. Before independence Congo had a surplus of cotton for export, but following the wars, was forced to import for her own needs; this was done largely through the United States aid program PL 480 under Title I. By 1968, Congo had recovered sufficiently to begin exporting again. Other crops such as manioc, corn, and peanuts—important to Congolese consumers for many years—are grown in rotation with cotton.

Many efforts are being made by the Government Ministry of Agriculture and Rural Development to encourage more Congolese to engage in agriculture, either through industrial concerns or individual farming. A very impressive experimental agricultural project, undertaken with Nationalist Chinese aid, is at N'sele, on the river some thirty miles from Kinshasa; this serves as an agricultural model for the country. Boats coming down the river at night are hailed by a blaze of light from the President's pagoda-style palace overlooking the N'sele farm (this is one of several presidential residences).

At the request of the Congo Government, the United Nations Development Program is involved in two other agricultural projects, the Agronomic Research Center at Yangambi (below Kisangani), and a demonstration agricultural and livestock program in the Ruzizi Plain in the Kivu, as well as a survey for fertilizer mineral deposits in the lower Congo.

N'Sele Agricultural Project, near Kinshasa

The universities and other institutions are also involved in research and training programs to improve the country's agricultural program; some projects are in connection with youth centers, such as the farm project of *Carrefour de Jeunes,* sponsored by the Church of Christ in Congo (E.C.C., Église du Christ au Congo) in Kinshasa. A group of some twenty young men spend a period of two years at the farm—which is some distance from the city—working and learning together under a highly qualified Congolese agricultural expert, using farming methods practical for village areas with a minimum of mechanical equipment. After the period of apprenticeship all the young men go out to rural areas of the country to set up similar pilot projects.

About two thousand different types of trees, including African oak, mahogany, ebony, red cedar, walnut, and wild rubber, attract a number of foreign industries; two United States plywood firms are among them.

Though fish are abundant in all the lakes and rivers—except for the volcanic waters of Lake Kivu—major fishing industry is still in development stage. The Government is setting up a model fishing port at Kinkole, neighboring the agricultural project of N'sele on the Congo River. Beginning with a broad paved boulevard christened "Zaire," down the center of the town, plans are underway to accommodate two thousand small fishing boats in the port.

Congo manufacturing is concentrated exclusively on domestic consumer needs; and must be supplemented by imports from abroad. At the International Industrial Fair, FIKIN, held in June, 1969, in Kinshasa, 168 Congolese firms had exhibits. Some sample companies: CHANIMETAL, concerned with metal construction, tools, shipping equipment; BRALIMA, beverages; TABACONGO, tobacco; UTEXCO, textiles; PLASTICONGO, plastics and rub-

Hostesses at International Fair, FIKIN, Kinshasa, June 1969

ber; BATA, shoes; BRICONGO, bricks and tiles; FORESCOM, lumber; ALUMINIUM CONGO.

With the increase of industrial activity, the demand for office and factory buildings, hotels and housing—especially in the major population centers—is at an all time high, taxing the construction industry to capacity.

Electric power consumption has risen considerably and as the hydroelectric project at Inga, in the lower Congo, progresses, there will be vast amounts available to develop contemplated steel and chemical complexes, an electric railway between Matadi and Kinshasa, and many other industrial projects throughout the country.

Freight and passenger traffic is straining far beyond capacity the Congo's transportation system; this has consisted mainly of railroads and the inland waterways of the Congo. Roads and railroads deteriorated during the turbulent years following independence; shipping equipment became obsolete; many new routes are needed to facilitate industrial development, tourism, and better communication for the Congolese people. To this end the Congolese Government, as well as U.S. AID, the World Bank, and the Common Market's European Development Fund are all investing large amounts of money in planning, construction, equipment, and maintenance for a modern transportation system by road, rail, river, and air. AID and the International Bank for Reconstruction and Development will help the Congo shipping company OTRACO and the Service of Navigable Waterways in improving and extending river operations. AID is also helping with modernization of airports, as the national airline Air Congo continues to improve its fleet. Plans for linking up existing rail lines with new ones to form a complete trans-Congo railroad system are being developed by a private consortium. The United Nations Development Program also has two special projects to improve transportation, one for national highway construction and maintenance, and the other a river transport study. This program is also developing a center for maintenance and repair of industrial equipment. While the contributions of U.S. AID and UND are helpful, they are far from adequate for the job that needs to be done. Much more foreign aid is needed to help the Congo realize its potential, both for its own people and for outsiders.

A recent U.S. Government economic study of the Democratic Republic of the Congo concluded that "the Congo could become the first country in Central Africa to reach self-sustained economic growth." The Republic is developing an economic system of its own that is a blend of American emphasis on private enterprise and the more socialistic systems, such as that of Britain, which have more government involvement. A new investment code announced recently by President Mobutu had attracted many firms from West Europe, America, and Japan; under this policy, important concessions are offered to companies investing in the Congo for the first time, as well as to established companies intending to develop their interests further. Thirty foreign nations participated in the International Industrial Fair (FIKIN), which was a joint undertaking of the Belgian and Congolese Governments.

While U.S. private business in Congo is increasing, U.S. AID funds are diminishing; U.S. Government help to Congo, though better than that for some other African countries, is minimal in proportion to its domestic expenditures. Some American projects include a 260-room Intercontinental Hotel in Kinshasa, a Union Carbide mining operation in the Eastern Congo, a Continental Grain Company flour mill in Matadi, and—the most recent—a $16-million tire plant to be built by Goodyear Tire and Rubber Company. (This is the first tire plant in the Congo and represents the largest foreign investment in consumer-product manufacturing in this country).

An American traveling through Congo today might be a bit disillusioned to find signs urging him to drink Coca-Cola, but back in 1877 Stanley might have appreciated such "a pause that refreshes."

12

Language and Communication

> "The islanders have not yet adopted electric signals but possess, however, a system of communication quite as effective. Their huge drums by being struck in different parts convey language as clear to the initiated as vocal speech...."

So wrote Henry Stanley describing the talking drums of the Ba-Ena tribe at Stanley Falls, after his journey there in 1877. Many other white men have been impressed and mystified with the efficiency of drum language, often used to relay messages to villages great distances away. Actually this is a very old art that until recently was a part of most Congolese boys' early training.

Dr. John F. Carrington, a British missionary now on the faculty of the Free University at Kisangani, is one of the few white men to acquire a real knowledge of drum language, probably as much because of his musical ability as his sensitivity and enterprise. After he told the Congolese that his father had been a member of an English country dance team, he was given a drum name which described his father leaping into the air, causing everyone to laugh until they ached: "*bosongo olimo ko nda lokonda ekese olongo lolikalika....*" For, as Dr. Carrington describes in his book, *Talk-*

ing Drums of Africa, drum language is based on the spoken language tones which are so important to all Bantu dialects. Drum messages always use word pictures with many distinguishing details. For example, "Don't worry" might be translated into Kele drum talk: "Take away the knot of the heart up into the air."

The same system can also be transferred to whistling. Schoolboys used to have great fun whistling out messages their white teachers could not understand: "Look out! The man with the scorched skin is on his way!" Congolese whistled out jokes or insults on *bula matadi* while their European masters thought the "natives" were very happy at their work. *Bula matadi,* or "Breaker of Rocks," was the name given to Stanley when he astounded the Africans with his conquest of the rocky area between Kinshasa and Matadi.[1] Afterwards, all government officers were named Bula Matadi.

The use of drums for messages has more or less died out in Congo today, except, perhaps in some remote areas, but the style and symbolism of the language is still an important tradition, especially evident in the work of modern young poets and writers.

There is so far no established evidence of a written language before that introduced by the Europeans, but some current studies of rock paintings and engravings in the lower Congo indicate there might have been a kind of writing generally known and used among the Bakongo perhaps during the period of the Kingdom of Kongo.

African languages were first written down in European form by Christian missionaries, the first published work being a Kikongo catechism prepared by Franciscan monks in 1557. As in the general education program, the missionaries—Catholic and Protestant— were the pioneers in providing literature in the Congo languages,

---

[1] Matadi = rocks

and it was fortunate that there were some genuine scholars among them. Often singlehandedly, they prepared grammars, dictionaries, and hymnbooks, translated the Bible, wrote textbooks as well as journals and pamphlets; they also organized literature distribution systems, the most effective being traveling bookmobiles reaching remote villages. Mission groups have also been instrumental in encouraging young Congolese writers, furnishing scholarships for specialized study at home and abroad. The University of Lovanium has developed a number of Congolese philosophers and writers.

As the Congo has emphasized national unity, the common language of French has been adopted for all writing, broadcasting, and general communication. However there are several African dialects spoken fairly widely: Kikongo, Lingala, Tshiluba, and Kingwana (a local form of Swahili). Special broadcasts in these languages and some literature and journals in each are necessary to maintain communication with more rural communities.

Going into a bookstore at Lubumbashi or Luluabourg you might find a collection of poems by Étienne Tshinday Lukumbi; a book on modern music by Michel Lonoh; a philosophical work on "mental decolonization" by Mabika Kalanda; or a collection of prize-winning works by Congo students, resulting from a literary contest sponsored by the Minister of Culture. All of these are in French, but there are also reading books in Lingala, Kikongo, and Tshiluba; books on health, child care, religious texts, geographies, and histories.

Newsboys all over the Congo sell copies of the popular illustrated weekly, *Zaire,* as well as other journals and newspapers. These are often tattered and worn and may be a year or so out of date, but it doesn't matter: everyone is hungry for reading matter. In 1970 some fifty newspapers, including about a dozen dailies, were listed in the Congo directory; many of these are in African dialects, and

Newspapers and Journals of Congo

National Radio studio, Kinshasa

some are published by church or business organizations. Some of the most widely read newspapers are *L'Étoile,* and *Présence Congolaise.* President Mobutu was the first editor of one of the papers still being published, *Les Actualités Africaines.* Most of these feature international as well as local news, and many encourage contributions from subscribers, often publishing poems or original compositions sent in by budding writers. *Le Courrier d'Afrique,* one of the few dailies not under government control, recently closed down, because of financial difficulties, shortly after its fortieth anniversary.

Electronic communication has made remarkable progress. Congo Radio (*Radiodiffusion Nationale Congolaise*) can now reach the whole country; programs are prepared in Kinshasa and airshipped via tape to regional stations located at Kisangani, Lubumbashi, Mbuji-Mayi, Bukavu, Mbandaka, and Luluabourg. These generally consist of news and music, in French, Kikongo, Lingala, Tshiluba, or Kingwana. European stations can also be heard on shortwave receivers. There are some small radio-broadcasting stations, as well.

Since the introduction of television to the Kinshasa area in 1966, video equipment has also been added to the much expanded independent Tel-Star station in Kinshasa, making it possible now for many people to watch live programs from the capital and from Brazzaville, as well as taped programs from abroad.

Local and international telephone service and the postal service are being expanded. Telecommunications within the Congo and between Congo and Europe and the United States are handled largely by radio. The United Nations Development Program is establishing a National School of Telecommunications in Kinshasa to train technicians and improve facilities.

In a recent address on national aims for communication, the

Train crossing the bridge at Kongolo

Minister of Information emphasized that the nation's networks could be a unifying and creative force if not used merely to entertain or distract, and if programming takes into account not only the more educated people of the city but also the man in the brush who would otherwise be cut off from the outside world. He urged planning cultural and educational programs that would have meaning for all the various kinds of people living in Congo.

And so through radio, television, and an ever-growing number of magazines and newspapers, the people of the Congo are literally tuned in to all that's going on in their vast country as well as in the outside world: the arrival of the American astronauts in Kinshasa; the latest "football" (soccer) match; housing needs in Congo; apartheid in South Africa; history of the ancient kingdom of Kongo; Mahalia Jackson, the American "La Callas du Gospel";

Congo River docks, Kinshasa

or the latest Congo threat to the South African singer, Miriam Makeba. A Kinshasa or a Lubumbashi journal might carry a farewell tribute to a popular American AID official, an illustrated article on Israel, or perhaps an interview with a modern African sorceress. Editors spend hours sorting out contributions from their readers, to add to their columns the latest scoop from Bandundu, Port Francqui or Luluabourg.

13

Art and Music

Jean-Marie N'Guinamau is one of Congo's leading sculptors: his works adorn the campus of Lovanium University, the O.A.U. Center on Mont Stanley, and his latest piece, "The Musician," will soon decorate the gardens of the presidential palace. He was acclaimed at the International Festival of Black Art in Dakar in 1966, at the Fifth Art Biennial of Paris in 1967, at the International Trade Fair (FIKIN) in Kinshasa in 1969, as well as an exhibit in Brussels in 1970. With all this recognition, N'Guinamau has only recently been able to afford his own studio in Kinshasa. For, important as art remains in Congo's tradition, it is not a money-making profession.

Some few artists such as N'Guinamau and the abstract painter, José Videira—whose works decorate halls and embassies of the United States, Europe, and Africa—are fortunate to make their living at art. Many others support themselves with other jobs while painting, carving, singing, or dancing in their off hours.

Whether they engage in it professionally, semiprofessionally, or just for fun, the people of the Congo are known for their art. For many centuries Congo carvings of wood and ivory, masks, cups, stools, and bas-reliefs in wood and metal have appeared in museums and private collections all over the world. Picasso's main

An artist in his studio

inspiration for the style he developed into cubism came from an exhibit of African art, including pieces from Congo, which he saw in Paris in the early 1900's. The African concept of creating not just what you see, but what you *know,* opened up an entirely new way of painting to the great artist. Recordings of Congolese traditional music and collections of their wide variety of musical instruments have also attracted international interest. Riding a taxi in Ghana or entering a store in Nigeria today, you are sure to hear Congo jazz, the favorite of all Africans.

When the *Apollo 11* American astronauts visited Congo in the fall of 1969, they were each given a chief's staff, the carved walking stick carried by all government dignitaries and anyone of importance. Aside from the significance of the gift, no one would want to leave the Congo without a souvenir of the carving for which it is world famous. Traditionally the carvings and masks are separated into specialties from different areas: Bakongo statuettes from the Lower Congo; ancestral portrait statues and cups from the Bakuba; the Baluba kneeling figures, chiefs, staffs, and colored masks; and the small masks of the Bapende.

In the past most of the carving and sculpture, as all artistic expression, was associated with religion. A statue representing an ancestor brings his spirit back and is an object for homage or worship; a carved cup may be used to hold a poison brew to test accused sorcerers. Also many objects are part of ceremonies connected with birth, marriage, or daily living. A Woyo bride, for example, receives as part of her trousseau a collection of carved pot lids, each illustrating a well-known proverb; when she wants to talk back to her husband she can simply pick up a lid and *show,* not throw it!

House decoration and design are highly developed in some areas, notably among the Bakuba. The Bakuba and the Baluba are also known for the beautiful palm raffia pile cloth that has been a specialty of Congo since the days of the ancient Kingdom of Kongo. Decorated mats, combs, head-rests, pots and jars, and all sorts of household objects—even body decoration—furnish examples of what would be judged fine art by foreign connoisseurs. But for the Congolese such "art" has always been a part of daily life.

As such traditions disappear with modernization, there are efforts by the Government and concerned individuals to preserve them. A museum and workshop has been established at Mushenge, in the art-rich area of the Bakuba. Similar efforts go on elsewhere to provide both a showplace and a training center for new artists: the Beaux Arts Museums in Lubumbashi and in Kinshasa; Prehistory Museum at Lovanium University; Museum of Leopold II at Lu-

ART AND MUSIC 113

bumbashi. The Tervueren Museum in Brussels, Belgium, contains one of the most complete collections of Congo art.

Recognizing that artists must also eat, some commercial outlets are being provided. The studios of the Berquin brothers in Katanga, specializing in painting and sculpture, with a number of Congolese artists engaged, exports 90 percent of its works to France and Belgium. Mission groups in some areas provide outlet shops for regional art. Many individual Congo artists have been able to sell their works to foreigners through the efforts of an American businessman living in Kinshasa, Mr. Maurice Alhadeff, who uses his

Carving ivory with modern tools

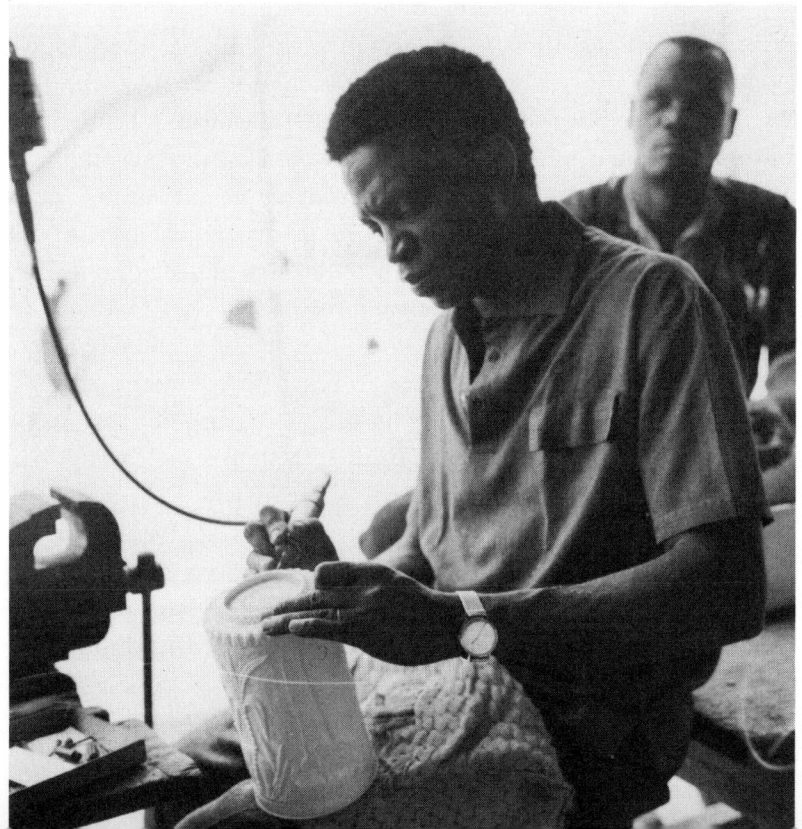

worldwide contacts on behalf of the artists and also provides materials and guidance. For his over fifty years of service to the country, in many causes besides art, Mr. Alhadeff was given the highest decoration of the Government, the *Ordre du Léopard* (Order of the Leopard). The Ivory Market of Kinshasa is a favorite tourist spot. Here individual vendors spread their wares out in an open lot on Boulevard 30 Juin, and carry on noisy bargaining far into the night. Depending on your resistance to sales pressure, as well as your ability to discriminate between what is known as "airport art" and the real art, you can find some beautiful things here at very good prices: ivory and wood carvings, statuettes, jewelry, paintings, and varied handcrafts.

"Congolese Music, Yesterday, Today and Tomorrow." This was the theme of the first conference on Congolese Music held at Kinshasa in December, 1968, to discuss the role of music in the Congo's modernization. For music, said one citizen, is so integrated into its life that "it envelops all the rhythm of development." While they are proud of their past—of the rich variety of instruments and traditional music that has delighted African music specialists—Congolese resent being treated as simply curios or as primitive people who cannot adjust to the modern world. A young man of Luluabourg or Lubumbashi wants no more to be confined to Lulua or Baluba songs than a New Yorker to Indian chants or hillbilly songs. The music at a university dance at Kisangani, Lubumbashi, or Kinshasa swings easily from pop to soul, to international jazz, to Congo jazz, on to the traditional Baluba "Kamulangu" (which has become a sort of national dance). Only in the "Kamulangu" would a foreigner be lost, for its stately steps are subtle and tricky.

The traditional music of Congo cannot be traced back as far as its sculpture, for, like the folktales and proverbs, it has been passed on orally from generation to generation. The earliest recordings are

Guitar player

not more than fifty years old; these were all made by foreigners who frequently did not know enough of language and customs to understand the full meanings, but were nevertheless fascinated with the sophisticated style and form. The Congolese themselves find it hard to distinguish today between pure traditional music and music with foreign influence. American folk tunes—which might actually have originated from Africa—have been given a Congo twist sometimes and called *music indigène* (native music); a saxophone or a guitar is just as comfortable for these musical people as a "tshisanji" (thumb piano) or a drum. It is their very ability to adapt and improvise that makes the popular music of Congo a sort of international potpourri, yet with a style all its own.

Recognizing the dangers of commercial success and too much foreign influence, the National Conservatory of Music and Drama, established by the Government, under the Ministry of Culture, has as its object fostering traditional African music and also teaching classical and modern Western music and instruments. Through this the school hopes to offer better tools to musicians trying to blend African and foreign forms and instruments; some are already doing this successfully, with little formal training.

Perhaps the best known adaptation of Congo music is the *Missa Luba,* which provided the musical theme for the movie, *If,* as well as a European film, on the life of Christ, *St. Matthew Passion.* Under the leadership of a Belgian priest, the men and boys of a choir at Kamina "composed" this Mass, setting the Latin words of the Mass to traditional rhythms of the Baluba. Father Bernard van den Boom, a Dutch priest now working at the youth center, *Carrefour de Jeunes,* in Kinshasa, composed *Missa Kwango* with a group of schoolboys who brought the melodies from their villages outside Kenge. Group composition is going on in many Congolese churches today, as African music becomes more meaningful in Christian worship.

The Kimbanguist church kept itself alive through its period of exile largely through its music. Composers and musicians are part of the official staff of the church today. Four of its nine main divisions of social work are: a theater group, a general choral group, a youth music group, and an organization of flutists.

Foreign and local record companies (such as Star, Philips, Ngoma) are doing a booming business in Congo discs, especially records of jazz and popular music. *Le Hit-Parade de Zaire* periodically lists the popular favorites, such as: the singer Franco with O.K. Jazz; Bombenga with Vox Africa; Bavon Marie-Marie with Négro-Succès.

Congolese, especially those living in the cities, are very much aware of the international entertainment world, which comes to them via movies, television, journals, and more and more personal tours. Within a period of a few weeks visitors might include a Moscow circus group, a Moldavian dance troop, a Senegalese theater ensemble, or perhaps an American pop star. Journals and newspapers are constantly interviewing new Congo artists: a sculptor, a painter, a musician, or a director of a theater group.

In his opening remarks at the Conference on Congolese Music, Minister of Culture Paul Mushiete concluded:

> "Our riches, we say, are not only in diamonds, in copper; our richness is not confined to mineral or vegetable resources. But it lies first of all in ourselves, its base is in our temperament, it is first an expression of our own feelings, and it is singularly this expression which must clothe the nationalism extolled by the New Regime . . . it is up to the artists and writers to bring the decisive victory."

14

Liberation of Women and Youth

The MPR (*Mouvement Populaire de la Révolution*) has as one of its stated objectives, "the liberation of women and youth."

Actually it was Lumumba, Congo's first Prime Minister, who was one of the first to take up the cause of women. His wife Pauline is said to have reminded him that Congo could not advance with educated and emancipated men alone, but must have the help of modernized women as well. The crowd that demonstrated at Lumumba's first major rally for independence, at Stanleyville, was largely female.

Mme. Sophie Lihau-Kanza, Minister of Labor, Housing and Social Affairs, is one of many women today to shatter the Congo's tradition of women in a subservient role. Glamorous and feminine to the last inch, Mme. Lihau-Kanza is on hand at every important government event and sets an example of efficiency and special insight into the affairs of the administration. She and others—women mayors, diplomats, soldiers, and some formidable policewomen— are forcing a reevaluation of the role of women in Congo.

Dr. Ina Dorine Nsumu, one of Congo's first women doctors, recently arrived with her doctor husband, after completing training in Belgium; they are the first medical couple in Congo. Dr. Thérèse-Henriette Malanda, Congo's first woman lawyer, also

"Miss Congo" Competition, July 1969

started out to be a doctor, but changed to law; she was one of three women to graduate in international law from the State University of Kiev in Russia (the other two were Polish and Yugoslavian, respectively), and is now with the Justice Department. The first female Congolese fashion designer has opened a studio in Kinshasa; "Miss Congo" represented her country at the Tokyo Expo; periodically a new singing star is proclaimed as a competitor to Miriam Makeba. There are increasing numbers of teachers, nurses, lawyers, and other professional women.

Not all Congolese women, however, lead such glamorous or useful lives. Indeed, for a great majority life is very hard, both in terms of physical hardships as well as in lack of respect and status.

Family life is still recovering from the deprivations of Congo's troubled years, during which many husbands and young men were killed. Families were separated or forced to relocate. There were years of starvation for some, permanently crippled bodies and minds for others. Many women have had to bear alone the burden of keeping themselves and their children alive. Some find men to support them, sometimes in legitimate marriage, but often in a common living arrangement with other "wives" or mistresses. There are not enough men to go around. Prostitution has become a necessity for the support of many families; young girls are sent into the city to solicit customers from the hotels and bars. In 1968 the Minister of Justice closed down all the so-called "houses of tolerance," where prostitution was openly practiced, but it continues under bare disguise, in well-known places.

Many organizations are working to meet these problems. The Marie Antoinette Mobutu Women's Center, named for the President's wife, has a rapidly expanding model program in the Limete commune of Kinshasa; this is specifically for helping uneducated, unemployed young women to become useful members of society. Here they learn practical homemaking skills, as well as literary subjects. Similar *foyers sociaux* (social institutions) are being run under government, church, UNESCO, and other sponsorship all over the country, to give women and young girls practical courses, help with child care, and guidance in self development. Some *foyers* have traveling units which reach remote villages.

Traditionally Congo women have assumed a great part of the responsibility for food raising and now they are asserting themselves in the agricultural sector, as well as other sectors, of the country's economy. Women are forming their own business associations or assuming leading roles in commercial organizations: Madame

Mbayu for example, serves as vice-president of Bukavu's Chamber of Commerce.

Tradition is not dead, by any means, and it can sometimes be put to good use, as demonstrated by a recent bride of Mayumbe, in Kongo Central. Before her marriage, the young woman had to pass the tests required of all brides of Mayumbe, where it is the custom to choose a wife not only for her beauty and domestic skill, but also for her devotion to field work. A few exceptions were made for the prospective bride, a city girl from Kinshasa. She was not required to spend a whole season with her future in-laws, plant and harvest an entire field, or carry a load of wood on her head, as in former times. She was received in her future husband's village like a queen, with gun shots, evenings of dancing, and riotous celebration. For an entire week people filed in to bring her gifts or simply to look her over. With all this, there still remained a test for her to pass: She had to hike a very long distance; the path assigned for her trial was up steep hills, through rocks, tangled vines, over many obstacles. Nevertheless she accomplished it and returned to receive cheers and shouts of joy from the villagers.

Back in Kinshasa with her husband, a government official, the successful bride was philosophical about it all.

"After all," she said, "for those who wish to get thin, this is much better than the special reducing salons in the capital!" Furthermore, she added, her field trip had taught her a great deal about how manioc was cultivated and made into the "fufu" that is such a popular taste treat in the city markets. She also got firsthand valuable information on food prices, on the palm industry, and on pineapple and coffee plantations, which could possibly be helpful to the Government.

Some of the social *foyers* combine programs for women with

122 THE LAND AND PEOPLE OF THE CONGO

special programs for youth, providing basic education, practical skills, and recreational activities.

Two international youth organizations, the Girl Guides and the Scouts, bring together children of many different nationalities and creeds. The Association of Guides of Congo, begun at Lubumbashi in 1937, and now numbering over seven thousand, held a "Thinking Day" at Kinshasa in early 1970 to celebrate the sixtieth birthday of the international organization (founded by the British Baden-Powell); a celebration which included Catholic European and Congolese students of the Sacre Coeur School, Protestants of the Martin Luther King Institute, Salvation Army, Muslims of the

Sports Parade, Kisangani

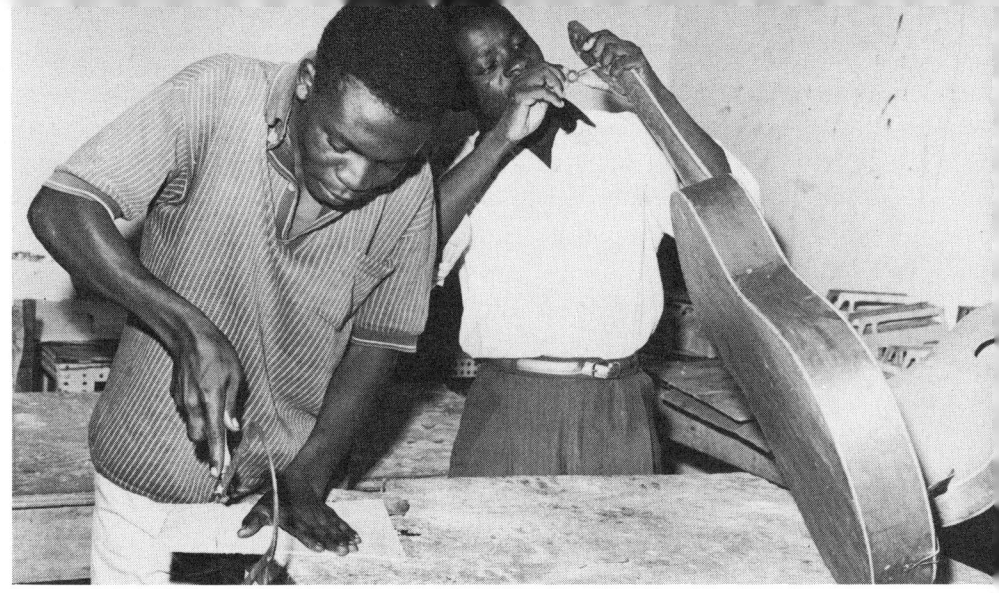

Homemade guitars being put together at Carrefour de Jeunes, Kinshasa

Agha Khan group. Catholic, Protestant, and Kimbanguist churches all have special youth programs.

An organization that is having increasing influence in combatting problems of juvenile delinquency due to school dropout and unemployment is the youth center, *Carrefour de Jeunes*. Begun five years ago under the sponsorship of the Congo Protestant Council, the original center at Kinshasa now has a full program open to all races and faiths, with the financial support of many leading business organizations of the capital, as well as foreign help. Its services include courses in typing and steno, sewing, English, as well as training in manual work, handicrafts, and music. It also has a placement service for locating young people in schools and jobs. There are several clubs, musical organizations, sports activities, library and restaurant facilities, a small orphanage, and a farm project outside the capital. Similar *Carrefour de Jeunes* centers are operating, or are underway, at each of the provincial capitals.

An important part of all youth programs—especially for boys—is sports. In this field, too, the Congo has excelled internationally. On their very first try outside the country, the "football" (soccer) team of the *Engleberts* walked off with the African championship. When Pierre Kalala, a national football hero, suffered a broken leg recently, the crush of his fans became such a threat to his recovery that he had to be hidden away.

Cycling, basketball, and javelin throwing are among other sports in which Congolese youth excel. Water sports are not as popular. Sunday afternoon at the "Stade," to watch a football game is a favorite family outing all over the country.

Though Congolese youth like a good time as well as anyone else, they are not all totally preoccupied with sports, music, and entertainment. Many of them—especially those who have had the privilege of higher education—are aware of their responsibility in finding solutions to problems of individual, national, and worldwide freedom. The young poet, Étienne Tshinday Lukumbi, thinks the ancient Congolese had some values worth preserving:

THE HUT OF MY GRANDFATHER[1]

Come from where machines roll,
Corrupted by worldly extravagances,
More vigorous, yet less believing,
Unripe and untrusting,
Such a beginner I was.
Entrance into this hut was my triumph.
Behind his bed, all juicy with age,

---

[1] "La Case de Mon Grand-Père," *Marche Pays des Espoirs*, Étienne Tshinday Lukumbi, p. 27; Présence Africaine. Translation from the French by Louise Crane.

Eyes more brilliant than silver,
Heart whiter than snow,
This mysterious being,
This father of uncounted years,
This old man, sweet and commanding,
Welcomes me in his frail arms.
He speaks of realities more convincing than all learned truth.
His sayings, his barely heard words give assurance to the doubter.
His teeth uncorroded by acids tell the life of a warrior.
His wise sayings exceed all the theories of school.
This broken-down hut still gives a welcome to the unbeliever fashioned by the West.
This hut, black with smoke and children's hands, still speaks truth.
My covenant with the West is broken.
Each day makes me think of this father of the father of my father.
Why ignore this enchantment of our people who are left free?

15

Life in the Country, Life in the Town

It would be impossible to describe typical life in Congo today, for it varies from group to group, both in the city and in the remote regions. Many people are extremely poor, others are relatively comfortable, and a very few are rich. Many of the poor people, especially those in the areas less accessible to planes and trains—such as the equatorial forests of the eastern province, or the Ubangi region—live much in the same way as their ancestors, eking out a living from hunting, fishing, and some rotational planting, living in grass thatched huts, trading at the village markets, participating in traditional ritual ceremonies. Scarcely anyone today, however, can escape the foreign influences that are ever creeping in, even to the farthest hut: a government or mission school or clinic, an airplane buzzing overhead, or a surveyor plunging through the brush in his Land Rover.

For Mukendi, a twelve-year-old Baluba boy in a village at the edge of a forest in West Kasai, life is very full. His village, located near a single railroad line from Luluabourg to Mweka, has about fifty inhabitants, living in small mud-walled houses on either side of a red dirt road lined with palm trees. Mango, papaya, and

A Congo family at the Otraco docks, Kinshasa

Children watching their mother pound corn in a mortar

banana trees, as well as more palms surround the houses, providing shade for the women pounding corn in wooden pestles, sifting manioc flour through wicker baskets or stirring "bidia"—a thick mush—in pots over open fires. On the grass roofs of the houses bits of hippopotamus meat and some forest caterpillars lie drying in the sun, filling the air with a strong odor. Goats, chickens, and swarms of scantily clad children chase each other through the trees, drawing a sharp reprimand from Mukendi's grandfather as they upset a gourd of palm oil lying ready for the "bidia." Having threatened to kill all of them, he returns calmly to his water pipe and takes a long draw while the women try to clean up the mess.

Mukendi's father makes palm wine to sell at the village market as well as to passengers going through on the train twice a week. Now that he is a man—Mukendi went through initiation rites several weeks ago—the son joins his father in work, climbing the palm tree to tap for wine, hunting for monkeys in the forest, helping the other men of the village to build neighbors' houses, or joining in as an observer at the palavers settled by the village elders.

Long before the shrill whistle announces the arrival of the train, Mukendi is established with his jars of palm wine at the choice spot along the track, ready to leap up to the windows and pounce on the first thirsty customer. Planted firmly beside him is his little sister Mbombo, a baby brother strapped to her back with a piece of brightly printed cotton. She holds a pan of peeled sugarcane and is nodding her head vigorously as Mukendi orders her to stick to the price they agreed on for the sugarcane. They both know it will be hard to hold out agaitnt the passengers—no one accepts the first price!

Both Mukendi and Mbombo sometimes attend the village school, conducted by a mission-trained teacher under a mango tree near the chief's house. But on train days, as on rain days, there is no school.

Jean Kalombo in Kinshasa has quite a different life. His father has a job with Socobanque. The Kalombo family live in Kalamu commune, in a modest concrete house with running water and electricity. To get to his office each day M. Kalombo has to take a city bus, often so crowded he cannot see out the window. Prices are very high in Kinshasa, so Mme. Kalombo is always looking for bargains at the Kalamu commune market or at the large city market, where individual vendors bring in fresh produce from the country. It is truly amazing how many people there are here waiting to sell you some fufu at an "extremely low" price simply out of "friendship"; they profess to be heartbroken if you turn them down. But Mme. Kalombo knows about this kind of friendship and passes on to another stall, perhaps less friendly but with better prices. If one has the money it is possible to buy almost anything in Kinshasa: grocery, butcher, and bakery shops offer a large variety of foreign imports, as well as local products, and there are many stores offering a wide choice of clothing or household supplies.

On occasional trips into the main shopping section of the city, Mme. Kalombo glances a little wistfully at an elegant boutique where a Congolese lady is trying on a high-fashion gown. She herself buys at other stores offering beautiful fabrics—many of them Congo-designed—at a considerably more reasonable price. All Congo women, whether dressed expensively or economically, have a unique sense of style, generally preferring the African fashion of long wrapped skirt with over blouse and towering headdress; the exotically printed cotton materials are sometimes cut in simpler European style shifts. M. Kalombo wears a short-sleeved, open-necked shirt worn loose over long trousers, generally in a heavy

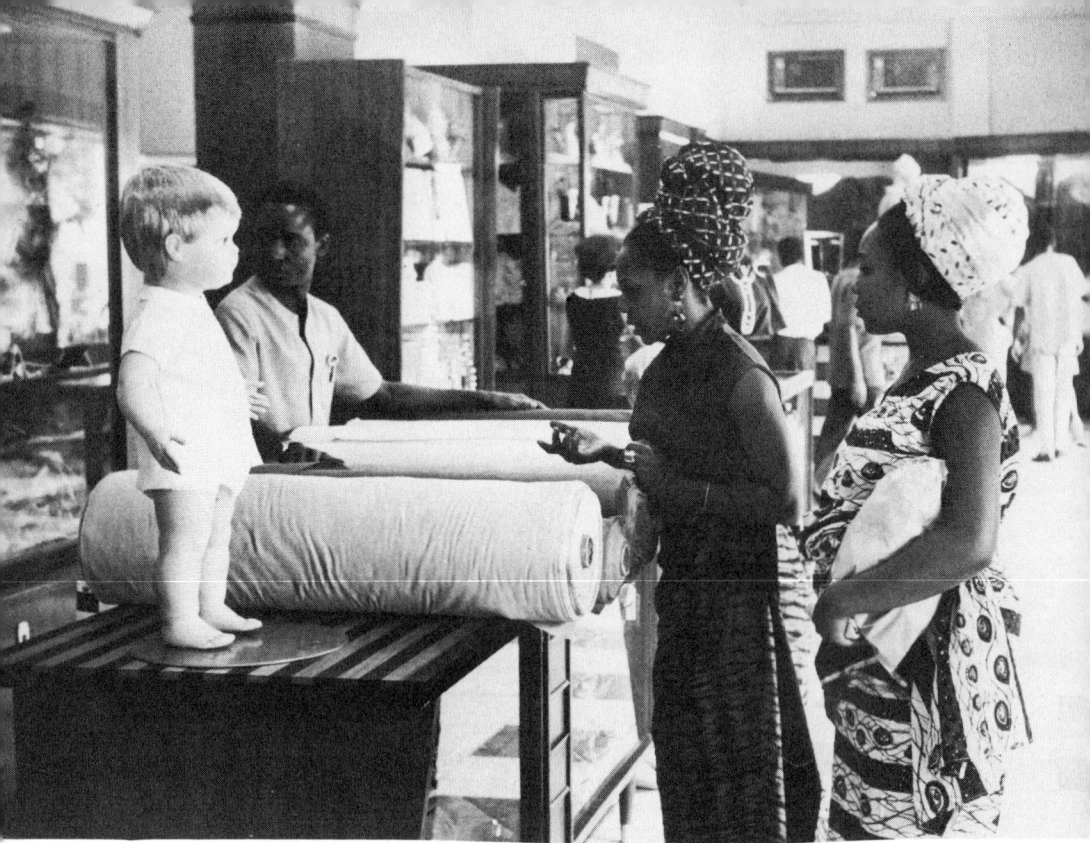

Selecting cloth in a city store

gray cotton. Government dignitaries and VIP's add to this a leopard fabric cap and a carved chief's staff. Jean dresses like all schoolboys, in tan-colored shorts and open-necked shirt; the current rage for footwear is very pointed shoes with rather high heels. Jean's shoelaces are deliberately *removed,* for the more flop the better!

Jean Kalombo goes to a government secondary school in Kalamu, where he is already specializing in studies leading to a law course. Football is his favorite sport, though he also likes basketball. Sometimes his school takes on the American School team in a basketball match. The American School is open to English-speaking children of all nationalities, and has some Congolese students.

Variations on Mukendi's life could be found in most of the rural regions of Congo—a Hima boy or girl in the east would spend a lot of time tending cattle; a Pygmy boy might live in the forest; or the son of a Wagenia fisherman, near Kisangani, finds his amusement and his living in the rocky rapids of Stanley Falls. City life similar to that of the Kalombos is common, perhaps on a simpler scale, in all the major cities and towns such as Lubumbashi, Kisangani, Luluabourg, Matadi, or Bukavu.

16

"Bring Me the Head and Feet with Which I Can March Forward!"

Traveling down the Congo in the old days, passengers leaned over the rails of the river steamer to find a dot in the water that might turn into a crocodile or hippopotamus. Today it is impossible to see anything but hyacinths—millions of clumps of beautiful purple hyacinths floating by. Beautiful, but the curse of the Congo! Planted in a private cove by a well-meaning foreigner in the 1950's, the hyacinths multiplied so rapidly that they have become a danger to navigation; thousands of zaires have been spent to get rid of them, but they still grow.

This is the story of the Congo: its continuous struggle to recover from misguided efforts of men. Sometimes it has been foreigners who have caused the trouble, some greedy and cruel, others well-meaning but blind. Sometimes its own people, with good and bad motives, have contributed to the problems.

Nevertheless the Congo flows on, ever mightier, ever changing, gathering all the forces of its separate branches—the volcanic waters of the Kivu, the muddy Kasai, the diamond-studded Lubilashi, the Kwilu, the Kwango, the Uele, the Sankuru—propelling them out to sea to join the waters of the world.

Parade of the MPR (Mouvement Populaire de la Revolution)

The country, like the river, can no longer remain divided within itself nor separate from the world. Even though, because of its tremendous size and the variety of its people, it is a giant task of unification, the Government is moving forward energetically to accomplish it.

With world attention focused on it and government and business concerns from everywhere coming to participate in the exciting opportunities offered by this rich land—opportunities made even more attractive by the new foreign investment policies initiated by the new regime—the young Government at Kinshasa must keep a tight rein on everyone involved in its development. The Congolese are fully aware of the selfish motive of many—both their own people and outsiders—who profess eagerness to cooperate with the *"Nouveau Regime."* Fresh memories of bloodshed, tribal warfare, meddling foreigners, betrayal by supposed friends, and the indignities of colonialism, make them wary. Yet they are not people to hold grudges or remain bitter. A few months after President Mobutu made a state visit to Belgium, King Baudouin returned to Congo to participate in the tenth anniversary of independence, June 30, 1970; he was greeted at Kinshasa with a 40-foot blue and yellow arch proclaiming, in French: "Belgians and Congolese—Let Us Unite." The President has made state visits to other countries aiding in Congo development, including a visit to Washington, D.C. in August, 1970.

Leaders and citizens of the Democratic Republic of Congo are both optimistic and realistic. Many hands are needed to build the new Congo, so whoever remembers and contributes—at least in some measure—to the goals of the new regime, is welcome, whether he is a Mongo serving as a government minister; a Mukongo or a Muluba operating the atomic reactor at Lovanium University; an American building the new television station; a Belgian or an Egyptian teaching; a Japanese planning the railway extension; or a Yugoslav directing the fisheries.

Congo is also aware of its responsibility to the rest of Africa in the continent's united struggle for freedom for all people. Besides the very large number of refugees from Portuguese oppressed Angola, there are refugees from Sudan, Rwanda, Rhodesia, and other countries who have found harbor here. The Democratic Republic of Congo has been a leader in organizing African countries to work together for common aims, and help to countries in particular need. Air Congo planes helped to bring relief to war-torn Nigeria at the end of civil hostilities in early 1970. Close by the presidential

President Mobutu with other leaders of African states

palace on Mont Stanley is a permanent center for the Organization of African Unity.

The young Congolese poet, Etienne Tshinday Lukumbi, sums up for himself and for many others his feelings about Africa and about his country in the poem, *"Terre Noble."*[1] Here is a translation of the closing lines:

> "Nyamuragira, Karisimbi, Kilimanjaro, are not all these
> giants powerful enough to withstand bombs and mines?
> Father of my ancestors, mother of our mothers,
> hope of our sons, open your arms and give milk to
> children without bread.
> We are thirsty for pure blood, underneath the watching moon.
> Give us your very flesh, your essence and your flavor!
> Indestructable you have remained through the centuries;
> today your sons call you. Go forward and find your place!
> (the reply):
> "I am here, protector of your gifts and of your goods,
> Go and bring back to me the head and feet with which
> I can march forward!"

---

[1] *Marche, Pays des Espoirs* by Étienne Tshinday Lukumbi, p. 15. Présence Africaine, 1967. Translation by Louise Crane.

Parade

Index

Academie des Beaux Arts, 91
Act of Berlin, 34
Actualités Africaines, Les, 107
Adoula, Cyrille, 52
African Travel Bureau, 19-20
Agriculture, 17, 19, 66, 96–99, 120, 121
Agronomic Research Center, 98
Air Congo, 18, 101, 134
Air service, 18, 20, 101, 134
Albert, King, 35, 37
Albert National Park, 16, 20
Alfonso I, King, 22–23, 24, 75
Alhadeff, Maurice, 113–114
ALUMINIUM CONGO, 100
American Presbyterian Mission, 77
Angola, 15, 22, 25, 134
Animals, 13, 16
Animism, 72–74, 80
Arabs, 28, 34
Art, 18, 110-117
Association of the Bakongo (ABAKO), 40–41, 42, 43
Association of Guides of Congo, 122–123
Astronauts, 108, 111

Baker, Sir Samuel, 29
Bakongo people, 21, 26, 40–41, 43
Bakuba people, 27, 112
Baluba people, 112
Banque Belge d'Afrique, 59
Banque du Congo, 59
Banque Nationale du Congo, 59
Bantu dialect, 18, 26
Bantu people, 18, 26, 65
Bargaining, 13
BATA, 100
Baudouin, King, 35, 37, 39, 40, 45–47, 134
Beatriz, Dona, 75–76
Beaux Arts Museums, 112
Belgium, 13, 14, 26–27, 33–37, 77, 81, 82, 87, 91, 92, 102, 113, 134; Congolese independence movement, 14, 38–47
Belgo-Congolese Community, 36
Boka, S., 57
Bolikango, 45
Boma, 20, 30
Bomanchala, Bo Kama, 27
Botanical gardens, 16
BRALIMA, 99
Brazza, Savorgnan de, 33
Brazzaville, 33
BRICONGO, 99
Brussels World's Fair, 39
Bukavu, 107

INDEX

Burton, Sir Richard, 29
Burundi, 15

Cão, Diego, 21
Carlson, Paul, 53
Carrefour de Jeunes, 123
Carrington, Dr. John F., 103–104
Cattle-raising, 66
Centre de Regroupement Africain (CEREA), 41
CHANIMETAL, 99
Children, 66–69
China, Nationalist, 97–98
Christianity, 22–25, 37, 40, 66, 74–81, 104–105
City life, 11–13, 129–131
"Civic merit" cards, 39
Civil service, 60
Climate, 15, 16
Cobalt, 17, 95
Cocoa, 97
Coffee, 17, 96
Common Market, 101
Communications, 103–105
Communism, 51–52, 53
Compagnie Géologique et Minière (GEOMINES), 96
Compagnie du Katanga, 34
Confederation of ethnic associations of Katanga (CONAKAT), 41, 43
Congo, Democratic Republic of: boundaries, 15; Constitution of, 58; geography, 15–16; government of, 55–62; independence, 14, 38–47; legal holidays, 59; provinces of, 57, 59; travel in, 18–20
Congo Free State, 34–35
Congo Information Service, 43
Congo My Country (Lumumba), 52
Congo Reform Association, 34
Congo River, 12, 13, 15, 21, 30, 33, 99, 132; source of, 15; travel on, 18–19

Congo-Afrique, 84–85
Congolese Bank Association, 59
Conrad, Joseph, 12, 34
Conscience Africaine, 40
Conservatoire National de Musique et Drame, 91
Continental Grain Company, 102
Copal, 17
Copper, 17, 23, 26, 28, 95
Corn, 97
Cotton, 17, 96, 97
Courier d'Afrique, Le, 107
Crystal Mountains, 15
Currency, 21, 59

Dancing, 80
De Gaulle, Charles, 42
Denmark, 91
Diamonds, 17, 94–96
Diangenda, Charles, 82
Diangenda, Joseph, 41, 82–83
Diviners, 72–73
Drums, 103–104

Ecole Nationale D'Administration (ENA), 60, 90
Education, 38, 39, 40, 43, 48, 49, 74, 78–79, 86–91, 99, 124
Elections, 60
Electric power, 100
Elisabethville, 38, 39, 50, 87
Elizabeth, Queen, 37
Equator, the, 15, 16

Family, the, 66–71, 120–121
Fifth Art Biennial of Paris, 110
Firearms, 22, 26
Fishing, 19, 66, 68, 99
Force Publique, 48, 49, 51
Ford Foundation, 60, 90
FORESCOM, 100
France, 26, 33, 48, 77, 92, 113
Free University of Kisangani, 79

Garamba National Park, 16
Gbenye, Christopher, 53
Germany, 29, 91
Ghana, 42, 49
Gizenga, Antoine, 51–52
Gold, 17, 23, 95
Goodyear Tire and Rubber Company 102
Great Britain, 28–32, 91, 102, 122
Great Rift Valley, 15
Greece, 29
Grenfell, George, 77

Hamitic people, 18, 64
Hammarskjold, Dag, 49, 52
Health, 36, 91–93
Heart of Darkness (Conrad), 12, 34
Henrique, Dom, 23
Hobgood, Benjamin, 79
How I Found Livingstone (Stanley), 30
Hungary, 29
Hunting, 66, 68
Hut of My Grandfather, The (Lukumbi), 124–125
Hydroelectric resources, 17

Ileo, Joseph, 52
Ilunga, Kibinda, 26
Institut D'Enseignement Medical, 91
Institut National des Mines, 91
Institut Pedagogique National, 90–91
Institut Polytechnique du Congo, 90
International African Association, 33
International Bank for Reconstruction and Development, 101
International Festival of Black Art, 110
International Industrial Fair (FIKIN), 99, 102, 110
International Red Cross, 91, 92
Iron, 26

Islam, 74
Ismaelite religion, 74
Italy, 29
Ivory, 17, 22, 23, 26, 34, 114

Jackson, Mahalia, 108
Japan, 102
Jazz, 18, 111, 114, 116
Jews, 74
Joao I, King, 75
Johnson Falls, 16
Jungles, 15

Kalala, Pierre, 124
Kalanda, Mabika, 105
Kalonji, Albert, 41, 51, 53–54
Kasavubu, Joseph, 40–41, 43, 45, 51–53, 82
Katanga, 34, 43, 48–52
Kikongo dialect, 18, 105
Kimbangu, Simon, 41, 75, 81–82
Kimbanguists, 41, 42, 81–85, 116
Kingwana dialect, 18, 105
Kinshasa, 11–15, 17, 18, 20, 54, 57, 83, 84, 108, 112, 114
Kisangani, 19, 20, 30, 107
Koli, Jean Felix, 61
Kongo, Kingdom of the, 13, 15, 21–25, 75, 112

Lake Albert, 15, 29, 65
Lake Bangwelu, 29
Lake Fua, 16
Lake Kivu, 15, 20, 99
Lake Mweru, 15, 29
Lake Tanganyika, 15, 29, 30
Language, 18, 22, 23, 27, 60, 79, 103–105
Leopold II, King, 13, 28, 30–35, 77, 95
Leopold III, King, 35, 37
Léopoldville, 33, 35, 39, 45, 50, 87
L'Étoile, 107

Lever Brothers, 96
Lihau-Kanza, Mme. Sophie, 118
Lingala dialect, 18, 105
Literacy, 36
Livingstone, David, 13, 28–30, 77
London Daily Telegraph, 30
Lonoh, Michel, 105
Lovanium University, 86–89, 105, 110, 112, 134
Lualaba Falls, 16
Luba empire, 26
Lubumbashi, 13, 17, 20, 107, 112, 113
Lukenge, King, 27
Lukumbi, Étienne Tshinday, 124–125, 136
Lulua Frères, 41
Lulua people, 41–42
Luluabourg, 13, 18, 39, 107
Lulualaba River, 30
Lumumba, Patrice, 15, 41–50, 54, 118; death of, 52
Lumumba, Pauline, 118
Lutumba, J., 57

McLean, Dr. David, 79–80
Makeba, Miriam, 108–109, 119
Malanda, Dr. Thérèse-Henriette, 118–119
Manganese, 17
Mangbetu people, 64
Manioc, 97
Manufacturing, 99–100
Marie Antoinette Mobutu Women's Center, 120
Marriage, 69, 121
Matadi, 19, 33, 38, 39
Matrilinear society, 69
Mayumbe forest, 16
Mbandaka, 107
Mbanza Kongo, 22
Mbayu, Madame, 120–121
Mbuyi-Mayi, 107

Medicine men, 72–73
Mining, 17, 20, 23, 26, 36–37, 94–96
Missa Kwango, 80, 116
Missa Luba, 18, 80, 116
Mobutu, Joseph, 21, 43, 51, 53, 54, 58–61, 85, 102, 107, 134
Mongo people, 66
Morrison, William, 77
Motion pictures, 116, 117
Mouvement National Congolaise (MNC), 41, 42, 43, 45
Mouvement Populaire de la Révolution (MPR), 53, 58–59, 60, 118
Msiri, 26
Mulele, 52
Munongo, 53–54
Museum of Leopold II, 112
Mushiete, Paul, 117
Music, 18, 21, 22, 45, 80, 84, 91, 105, 107, 110–117

National Anthem, the, 55–57
National Congolese Army (ANC), 18, 59
National Conservatory of Music and Drama, 116
National Institute of Building and Public Works, 91
National Insurance Association, 59
National School of Telecommunications, 107
New York Herald, The 29, 30
Newspapers, 105–107
Ngola, King, 25
N'Guinamau, Jean-Marie, 110
Nile River, 15, 29
Nilotic people, 18, 64–65
Nkrumah, President, 42
Nsumu, Dr. Ina Dorine, 118

Ordre du Léopard, 13, 114
Ordre du Zaire, 21

Organization of African Unity, 14, 136
OTRACO, 19, 101

Palm products, 17, 96
Parti National du Progrès (PNP), 41, 43
Patrilinear society, 69
Peanuts, 97
People's Republic of Congo, 15, 22
Picasso, Pablo, 110–111
PLASTICONGO, 99
Population statistics, 18, 65
Portugal, 15, 21–25, 28, 134
Prehistory Museum, 112
Présence Congolaise, 107
Prostitution, 120
Proverbs, 17, 63, 114
Ptolemy, 16
Pygmies, 16, 18, 29, 63, 64, 66

Radio, 107
Radiodiffusion Nationale Congolaise, 107
Raffia cloth, 24
Railways, 18, 37, 100–101
Rain forests, 15
Religion, 41, 72–85, 112, 122–123; *See also* names of religions
Rhodesia, 134
Roads, 18, 33, 101
Round Table Conference, 43–44, 45
Royal Geographical Society, 28–29
Rubber, 17, 34, 96–97
Rural life, 13, 126–129
Ruwenzori Mountains, 16
Rwanda, 15, 53, 64, 134
Ryckmans, André, 36, 49–50
Ryckmans, Pierre, 35–36

Salt, 26
Schweinfurth, George Augustus, 29
Sheppard, William, 77

Silver, 23, 95
Slavery, 23–24, 26, 33, 34, 37, 75
Smuggling, 94, 96
Soap, 17, 96
Société d'Enterprise et d'Invessements du Beceka (SIEBEKA), 96
Société Generale des Congolais des Minerais (GECOMIN), 96
Société Generale des Minerais (SGM), 96
Société Minière de Bakwanga (MIBA), 96
Speke, John Hanning, 29
Sports, 124
Standing Commission for the Protection of Natives, 36
Stanley Falls, 20, 30
Stanley Pool, 13, 30, 33
Stanley, Sir Henry, 13–14, 20, 28–33, 102, 103
Stanleyville, 39, 43, 52, 53
Strikes, 38, 52
Sudan, 134
Sudanese people, 18
Sugar, 97
Swahili dialect, 18, 65, 105
Syndicat Minière d'Étain (SYMETAIN), 96

Talking Drums of Africa (Carrington), 103–104
Tanzania, 15, 61
Taxation, 34
Tea, 97
Telephone service, 107
Television, 107, 117
Terre Noble (Lukumbi), 136
Tervueren Museum, 113
Thant, U, 52
Theater, 91, 116
Through the Dark Continent (Stanley), 30
Thysville, grottoes of, 16

INDEX

Tin, 17, 95, 96
Tip, Tippo, 28
Tourism, 16, 101
Tribes, 43, 44, 48, 49, 64–66, 99; groupings and percentages, 18; *See also* names of tribes
Tshiluba dialect, 18, 105
Tshombe, Moise, 26, 41, 43, 45, 49, 50, 52–53
Tshopo Falls, 16
Tuckey, Captain, 28–29

Uganda, 15
Unemployment, 42
Union Carbide Company, 102
Union Minière du Haut Katanga, 17, 38, 95–96
Union of Soviet Socialist Republics, 51, 119
Unions, 38, 40
United Nations, 38, 41, 49, 52, 87, 91, 98, 101, 107
United States of America, 35, 49, 53, 77, 87, 91, 97, 99, 101, 102, 107–110, 134
Université Libre, 88–90
Université Officielle du Congo, 87, 88–89
Upemba National Park, 16
Uranium, 17, 95

UTEXCO, 99

Van Bilsen, Professor, 40
Van den Boom, Father Bernard, 116
Van der Meersch, Walter Ganshof, 45
Victoria, Queen, 29–32
Videira, José, 110
Virunga Mountains, 15
Vita, Kimpa, 75–76
Volcanic mountains, 15, 20
Vyncke, Aimé, 77

Wages, 39
Watts, André, 21
Watusi, 16, 63, 64
Wildlife sanctuary, 16
Women, 66–69, 118–122
World Bank, 101
World Council of Churches, 84
World Health Organization (WHO), 91, 92
World War II, 38

Yellela Falls, 29
Youth, 122–125

Zaire, 86, 105
Zambezi River, 15, 29
Zambia, 15, 61
Zande people, 64
Zinc, 17, 95

About the Author

Louise Crane was born at Luebo, in the Kasai area of the former Belgian Congo, where her parents were American Presbyterian missionaries. She received her early education in the Congo, and earned her bachelor of arts degree from Queens College, Charlotte, North Carolina; her bachelor's of religious education from the Presbyterian School of Christian Education at Richmond, Virginia; and her master's of sacred music from Union Theological Seminary, New York.

Miss Crane now makes her home in New York where she teaches, writes, and lectures. She has made professional appearances as a singer and lecturer on the Congo and Congo music. She also serves as a consultant with the Human Affairs Research Center, and has presented a number of programs on Africa at schools and clubs.